CRITICAL INCIDENT MANAGEMENT

D1712290

CRITICAL INCIDENT MANAGEMENT

Rod Paschall

OI
CJ
**The University of Illinois
at
Chicago**

Library of Congress Cataloging-in-Publication Data

Paschall, Rod, 1935-
Critical incident management / Rod Paschall
p. cm.
Includes bibliographical references and index.
ISBN 0-942511-54-9
1. Crisis management. I. Title
HD49. P37 1992
658.4—dc20

92-54159
CIP

ISBN: 0-2-942511-54-9
LOC: 92-054159

Manufactured in the United States of America

55653

CONTENTS

CRITICAL INCIDENT MANAGEMENT

INTRODUCTION

What follows is not just about surviving; it is about succeeding while a threatening incident or crisis is occurring. Mostly, the techniques, procedures, and principles outlined are addressed to the public or private institution, corporation, or organization in a crisis. Although much is directly applicable to crisis management, the scope extends beyond the crisis in which all is gambled and all may be lost. The most immediate object is to outline the principles, techniques, and procedures that will assist an institution in avoiding a potentially ruinous crisis. If, however, a crisis does occur, these same principles, techniques and procedures will be helpful in allowing an institution to prevail. When an "incident" becomes "critical," the incident can potentially become a crisis, and subsequent critical incident study, planning, practice, and management are warranted. "An institution is not simply concerned with surviving a crisis. It will want to avoid it to either continue or gain success, not just to survive. In order to survive, people within the institution must avoid trouble. If they find themselves in jeopardy, they should know how to overcome their difficulties as soon as possible. Successful critical incident management is important."

A critical incident or a crisis is simply a sudden, unexpected event that poses an institutional threat suggesting the need for rapid, high level decision-making. A critical incident is of lesser magnitude than a crisis. Both occur all the time. They are experienced by businesses, police departments, municipal and state governments, and the highest echelons of national government. Some claim that the definition of a crisis includes the inherent possibility of either a successful or unsuccessful outcome. People experiencing a crisis find themselves wholly focused on avoiding disaster. A critical incident or crisis hardly ever results in a successful outcome. No matter how well handled, it rarely results in higher profits for a business or more public confidence for some shaken echelon of government. "Normally, the best that people can expect is that the crisis will end quickly; losses will be minimized; and the organization will emerge a bit more experienced, a bit more resilient and maybe a lot wiser than it had been. However, the worst can happen. An institution can be plunged into the middle of a Chapter 11 bankruptcy proceeding, be ruined in a major liability suit, be forced to dismiss most of its employees. Bankruptcy, legal suits, and lay-offs occur all the time.

In America, critical incidents and crises were so common during the late 1970s and early 1980s that crisis management became an industry. Books on the subject were published in rapid succession. Would-be crisis management consultants were liberally distributing business cards and devising all kinds of "get smart quick" courses and advisory services. In 1978-1979, the "second oil shock" occurred. The price of oil again increased rapidly, as it had done earlier in the decade. American economic growth dropped to dangerous lows. President Jimmy Carter sat in front of a television camera, wore a sweater, and with a crackling fireplace as a back drop, he lectured his country about conserving energy. His message was about crisis. Some say his message started the crisis concerning oil. Later, he seemed to spend more and more time soberly telling Americans about the Soviet invasion of Afghanistan, the U.S. boycott of the Moscow Olympics, the seizure of the U.S. Embassy in Iran, and the failed rescue attempted to free American hostages in Tehran.

Crises seemed to be everywhere, affecting everybody. In 1978, the Firestone Tire Company came under attack. The corporation was desperately trying to prove its 500 Series of steel-belted radial tires were not the cause of thirty-four deaths as was being suggested by the National Traffic Safety Administration. In March, 1979, the near melt-down of a nuclear reactor at Three Mile Island in Pennsylvania raised fears of thousands of deaths and hundreds of square miles of contaminated soil. During the next year, Procter & Gamble hastily withdrew its Rely tampons from thousands of retail stores throughout the United States. The firm began defending itself against an increasing number of costly suits, charging that the company was responsible for women's deaths due to toxic shock syndrome. In 1982, Johnson & Johnson found itself the victim of a product-tampering campaign by an alleged psychopath who was killing the company's customers by lacing the popular headache remedy, Tylenol, with cyanide. In 1984, more than 2,000 people died in Bhopal, India; they were victims of a disastrous release of the deadly gas, methyl isocyanate, at Union Carbide's pesticide plant. With these crises in government and business, including a number of bloody terrorist incidents, crisis management became a trendy concept.[2]

The initial books and advice on crisis management had several limiting characteristics. Although most of the writing and consulting was aimed at making money, most of the books and articles were concerned with commercial applications. Lessons learned by government in crisis were largely ignored; as a result, valuable material was overlooked. The focus of much of this literature was upon the major catastrophe, the big company, and the well-paying customer. Consequently, proposed solutions were often expensive. The small or mid-sized company and the mid-sized echelons of government found recommended remedies beyond practical realization. Most of the literature and thinking was produced in the economic boom era of the 1980s, a period when adding more employees, sending people to training courses, or hiring additional consultants did not seem unreasonably expensive. With the arrival of the 1990s, a time of "downsizing," slashed budgets, staff reductions and early retirements, the standard suggestions for crisis management in the 1980s appeared beyond the budgetary limitations of all but the very large corporations.

Instead of being concerned with large corporations, this book will offer suggestions and solutions for small or mid-sized companies as well as mid-sized federal, state, or local governments. The focus is using critical incident management to approach seemingly mid-sized or small problems before they become serious and threatening. Rather than proposing the addition of new organizations to deal with a critical incident or a crisis, a concerted effort has been made to use people within organizations that already exist.

Some thought should be given to the phenomenon of crisis and the fundamental meaning of a critical incident. They are threatening, because when they are first perceived, they seem mysterious, new, and unusual. They portend future change which may seem unreal. It is imagined change that can be most feared and threatening. Successful people and institutions often abhor change, because they fear they have not adapted to the changing conditions they foresee. They do not want to be misfits in a different environment or a new situation. A natural, easily understood human instinct urges people to cling to the familiar, comforting world where they have survived. Change is not only feared; it can become a crisis, a critical incident in itself.

Yet people, particularly competitive Americans, can be very adaptive to new environments and differing conditions. In many ways, America is a land peopled by misfits, who could not adjust in other societies. Almost eighty-five percent of all Americans have ancestors who voluntarily uprooted their lives in other countries, transported themselves to an unfamiliar land, and thrust themselves into a uncertain future. Many Americans seem to know instinctively that the first step to survival and to success is change. Americans are a relatively new tribe, whose only common characteristic seems to be a desire for change. Unlike many other populations, Americans know there is nothing more normal than change. No matter what the facts may actually reveal, Americans are apt to equate change with progress.[3] It is just as well they do, because in the 1990s, there is likely to be much change in America.

2

PAST AND FUTURE CRISES

In the coming years, corporations, businesses, law enforcement organizations, and local and state governments will face more critical incidents and crises than they have in the past. Some causes of these crises include economies of scale, the steady increases in population, America's deteriorating physical infrastructure, the absence of a national energy policy, and technological developments. Crises may also be affected by potential legal actions, the mobility of populations, trade competition, and journalistic trends. Although threatening events may occur, the individual well-being of Americans can improve. The life expectancy of U.S. citizens will probably be lengthened.

CRITICAL INCIDENT MANAGEMENT 9

Although there has been almost a decade of falling or stagnant rates of per capita income for eighty percent of Americans, incomes may slowly increase. Meanwhile, however, the health and well-being of our institutions are increasingly threatened. U.S. companies are facing growing competition, because inexpensive efficient transportation is available globally. Large, fast container ships, material-handling equipment, huge commercial cargo aircraft have made international trade an ever expanding component of the overall American market. Many foreign business competitors have been able to transport high quality goods at lower costs than U.S. businesses. The American automobile industry has not been the only U.S. business to become less competitive in international markets. Businesses manufacturing clothing, steel, construction equipment, and electronics are losing markets. Some groups in American agriculture have also lost markets. When the European Community, the powerful twelve nation economic consortium, begins to realize the advantages of bargaining as a single nation, it will shift production to its most efficient companies and combine the talents and skills of its most productive industries. Some of the results can already be seen as Americans face stiff competition from the new Europe. That American business is already confronted with competition from Japan, Taiwan, South Korea, Hong Kong, and Thailand means only that competition is going to intensify.

International competition will not economically destroy America; the nation may thrive in the coming years. Both Japan and Western Europe have declining populations and the expenses of labor will increase steadily for them. The modest population increases and continuing influx of immigrants ensures a healthy supply of American workers. U.S. industrial productivity has been unevenly but gradually improved for nearly a decade, and workers have generally been restrained with wage and benefit demands. The European Community may look menacing, but so does the emerging North American economic confederation, a consolidation of Mexican labor and oil, U.S. industrial plants, and Canadian talent and resources. Eventually, the North American market may prevail.

However, time to overcome serious challenges is growing short. One competitor is quick to take advantage of another's mistake. The era of growing competition produces ever diminishing profit margins. The financial reserves to battle a lengthy liability suit, to pay for repairs after a severe storm, or to survive a sudden price war are becoming smaller, not larger. As a result, any crisis or critical incident can destroy an otherwise healthy corporation. Businesses that could have survived a long period of stress just ten years ago are becoming every day a bit more vulnerable to unpredictable events.

For several years during the early and late 1970s, cartel-driven, high oil prices staggered the U.S. economy, stifled growth, drove some businesses to failure, and caused unemployment. The price of oil may increase again when the United States is more dependent on foreign oil now than it was fifteen years ago. In the 1970s, the U.S. imported forty-four to forty-eight percent of its oil; in the 1990s, the U.S. will import sixty percent of its petroleum. The nation survived the 1990-1991 Gulf War without a major energy emergency only because Arab allies agreed to increase production. Sadly, as in the case of the earlier oil shortages of the 1970s, Americans seemed to ignore the need for an intelligent energy policy. About the only difference between the oil crisis of the 1970s and one that might happen in the 1990s is that a new crisis is likely to be more serious and damaging than it was fifteen years ago.

How prepared is American business for the critical incident—the war, the tornado, the deadly accident, the massive criminal extortion, or the huge liability suit? Two polls, one by the crisis management expert, Steven Fink, and the other by Western Union, were taken in the mid-1980s. In the late 1970s, the nation's largest companies, the Fortune 500, began a substantial, widespread effort to plan for unexpected, potentially threatening catastrophes. Unfortunately, after five years, only half of these companies had crisis management plans. Fink's poll indicated that almost ninety percent of the companies fully expected some sort of crisis and about seventy-five percent of them thought their own corporation was vulnerable. However, more than forty percent of those companies that had survived a crisis in the past still had no plan.[4] Consequently, the corporation leaders in 250 of the businesses in the nation are expecting future crises but cannot be bothered to plan in advance how to confront them.

Local and state public officials in the 1990s are likely to face as many troubles as business leaders. During the 1980s, the federal government shifted its responsibilities to states and local governments. Federal matching funds and revenue sharing have been reduced. The U.S. government has raised standards for Medicare, transportation, and welfare benefits, without providing the necessary funds to meet those standards. Increasingly, state and local governments had to provide funding by increasing taxes in the summer of 1991. Inevitably, more tax increases will be needed. Accompanying these tax increases is another trend toward more damage claims and money seeking litigation in cities and states. Public officials can be and are sued for failing to deliver health and welfare benefits. These same officials can be taken to court for not having adequate and appropriate emergency-management plans. State and local officials can be held liable if they are incompetent in their performances during a critical incident. Recent court rulings provide case law for these officials, and these rulings will be increasingly used to reinforce a growing number of plaintiffs' claims against public officials in the coming years. [5]

State and local officials are increasingly finding the country's physical infrastructure in disrepair. Unlike Europe where roads, canals, bridges, sewers and dams were built of stone over a period of three centuries, the U.S. physical infrastructure was constructed of concrete from 1900 to the 1950s. Now, that concrete is cracking. It has been estimated that forty-seven percent of America's bridges are in rapid deterioration. At current rates of repair, it would require eighty years to repair them—an impossibility because many bridges would collapse during that time. To avoid potential disaster, it is essential to find funds to repair the infrastructure immediately. Between 1970-1990, the U.S. only spent three-tenths of one percent on infrastructure compared to Japan spending five percent and Britain spending 1.8 percent. It is believed that the U.S. has a three trillion dollar task of repairing its roads, bridges, canals, sewers and dams. [6] To raise three trillion dollars is the thankless job of state and local political leaders.

The potential for future crises will probably increase due to international travel, population growth, and the economies of scale. Chemical, pesticide, and fertilizer plants are being consolidated or rebuilt for purposes of economy. The magnitude of a disaster at one of these new large facilities will be deadly. Twenty years ago, the crash of a large jet airplane was extremely rare because few large passenger aircraft were in service. Now, a 747 plane crash might well result in 200 deaths rather than the fifty to a hundred deaths in a smaller plane. Often, it is more economical for airlines to use a large aircraft rather than a small one, but more human lives are at risk in larger airplanes. Many lives could be endangered by catastrophes in recently constructed auditoriums, coliseums or shopping malls. Economies of scale make it profitable to build big, while construction flaws and natural disasters can jeopardize more people than they did previously.

People can also expect a continuation of the growth in rapidly spreading debilitating diseases and bizarre events caused by irrational people. The steady increase in international travel ensures that viral borne illnesses will spread quickly throughout the world with little warning. Travel and tourism has made even the most remote and isolated peoples easily accessible, and some of these people host diseases that have not been experienced by other populations. Although the inhabitants of remote settlements may have developed an indigenous immunity to a virus, tourists and visitors may not. Recurrent and occasionally deadly influenza epidemics and AIDS are examples of communicable diseases that can cause major crises. The increase in population can contribute a larger number of irrational people on earth. One irrational person—a murderer, a terrorist, or a kidnapper—can create a critical incident. Although it is difficult to evaluate human behavior, ample reason exists to believe that the steady, stressful growth of populations provides more irrationality today than twenty years ago.

Trends in journalism can threaten or ruin a corporation or some political leader's public administration. During the late 1980s and early 1990s a steady deterioration in civility was shown by print and broadcast media toward American business leaders and politicians. Some thoughtful journalists have cited the improprieties extended to both Senator Gary Hart and his entourage by reporters who disclosed his sexual excesses in 1987. Former guidelines, allowing editors to omit titillating details of a presidential candidate's personal life, were jettisoned. Other concerned journalists cite the Vietnam War as the beginning of a decline in professional standards in journalism. The noted reporter and columnist, Georgie Anne Geyer, contends that in that war journalists discarded the concept of reporting the facts in favor of new objectives: making personal judgments and advocating causes to change society.[7] In both print and television journalism, "tabloid-style" news reporting became commonplace. If a corporate officer or a politician makes a moral or legal mistake, they risk having their mistakes exposed as they never would have been. Moreover, because more laws are passed every year without a commensurate amount of legislation being deleted, there is a growing chance mathematically that a prominent public person will make a legal error or commit a crime. With "tabloid style" journalism, truth, balance or fairness will not matter; in the 1990s, public figures can unfortunately be ruined easily by rumor, false accusation, and innuendo.

Who would have doubted the growing importance of the small, easily concealed videocamera in recording misdeeds and indiscretions. Technology is going to provide a great deal of amateur film footage of shocking events in the coming years. Technology is producing portable catastrophes. During the Gulf War, a Kuwaiti resistance fighter hit and downed a large Iraqi passenger jet with a hand-held, anti-aircraft missile. In a year, will this kind of missile be on the shoulders of terrorists on airplanes, in business offices, and at politicians' parades? Similar weapons are being manufactured for effective use against tanks, and it is likely they might be used by terrorists attacking office buildings, liquid natural gas transporters, hazardous materials storage areas, and other targets. There are irrational human beings, and their weapons of destruction and death are more accurate, more lethal and more available than ever.

U.S. industry has been increasingly plagued with damage suits and expensive litigation. In August 1991, Vice President Dan Quayle challenged America's lawyers to find ways to make their profession less damaging to U.S.

competitiveness. Mr. Quayle asked why America, with only
five percent of the world's population, must have seventy
percent of the world's lawyers. Neither the question nor the
challenge was surprising. The costs of litigation are not
unknown to America's economic and industrial rivals. They
do not have to pay the costs of that litigation as their U.S.
counterparts do.

In 1978, the U.S. led the world in building 18,000 pleasure
and business airplanes. Ten years later, America
manufactured only 1,143 light aircraft. The dramatic decline
of a former money-making industry was caused by personal
injury suits. The suits provoked insurance companies to
increase their liability fees from an average $300 per aircraft
engine to more than $16,000. The result has been lost jobs, a
growth in foreign built pleasure and business aircraft
imported into the U.S., and a series of deadly crashes
involving the planes built abroad. Former Chief Justice
Warren E. Burger contended that suits against the nation's
doctors have increased 300 times since the early 1970s
causing physicians' liability insurance costs to increase thirty
times. He also cited the fact that American trial lawyers
earned more than $13 billion in personal injury awards in
1990; some lawyers demanded and received as much as
$1500 per hour for their services. Lawyers managed to take
$83 billion from the nation's economy in 1989, gaining
better than a hundred percent increase in only six years.[8]
There is nothing to slow this large increase in American
corporate legal costs. In fact, there is every indication that
lawyers' fees will be a greater burden to businesses in the
1990s. In answer to the Vice President's question, excellent
corporate lawyers can make a great deal of money in a
competitive, capitalistic nation. The next unasked question
is: when the fees of those lawyers impede the
competitiveness of that nation, what must be done?

U.S. citizens are specialists at solving their problems. Americans have over the years secured their well-being and have mitigated catastrophes due to recurring natural disasters. In September 1900, 6,000 Texans lost their lives during a hurricane. They built a sea wall and fifteen years later, only 275 deaths occurred in a similar storm. Later, Texans and people in other disaster prone settlements along the U.S. East Coast established radio-warning services and air spotting procedures to further reduce deaths in hurricanes. Radar systems were built, and evacuation was planned to be used when necessary. Despite a large growth in population along the U.S. eastern seaboard, deaths per $10 million of inflation adjusted storm damage actually dropped from 166 during the 1920s to fewer than two in the 1960s. When Americans decide to organize themselves to solve a problem or overcome an obstacle, their world can become less menacing, more tranquil, and more cost-effective.

3

ORGANIZING FOR A POTENTIAL CRITICAL INCIDENT

Enough organizational experience exists in dealing with a sudden and threatening situation that it is possible to draw some sensible conclusions. Although the federal government may not present a good example of thrift or efficient operations, it can provide some lessons on how to deal with critical incidents and crises. From the world of industry and commerce much can be learned from actual cases, many from just five or ten years ago. Although there may be few specific details, causes, or results that are common to these past cases, they usually share one element. Most critical incidents are under the supervision of a designated organization, and in some cases, a previously designated, specially trained team. Substantial knowledge exists on how various organizations have worked to get unexpected and menacing circumstances under control. It is possible to examine what happened, select what worked, discard what did not work, and choose a reasonable, generalized structured approach to deal with critical incidents and crises.

U.S. national security provides some of the best examples of managing critical incidents and crises. Before the advent of the literature of crisis management in the 1980s, everyone had their own definition of a crisis. President Dwight D. Eisenhower said it seemed he was asked to handle at least one crisis every day. A 1976 Brookings Institute study listed 215 international crises between 1945 and 1975, approximately seven per year. The Brookings estimate substantially agrees with an informal estimate by former Secretary of State Dean Rusk who said that an average of eight crises occurred every year. Another study by the Strategic Studies Institute in Pennsylvania listed only those crises in which the U.S. President was required to make a decision whether or not to employ American armed forces. The President was involved in approximately one serious incident per year from 1945 until 1974.[9] Nevertheless, a substantial data base of U.S. government's management of crisis and critical incidents exists during the era of the Cold War.

The American organization that was to deal with the many critical events during 1945-1989 was established within five years following the end of World War II. The organization was comprised of the National Security Council, the Central Intelligence Agency, and the Department of Defense. The bitter memories of the sudden and devastating attack on Pearl Harbor remained. Throughout World War II, the failings of the U.S. Government so vividly and tragically demonstrated on December 7, 1941 were studied by a number of committees and bodies of inquiry. At the end of the war, most deliberations were finished. It was generally agreed that the ordinary conduct of business in Washington and of the institutions primarily oriented toward foreign affairs would have to be redirected or reorganized. It was determined that the Cabinet, the traditional high council of the executive branch, was not an effective forum for dealing with dangerous foreign crises. Although the Postmaster General, the Secretary of Agriculture, and the Secretary of Interior were in the Cabinet, no military or naval officer served in it. During a serious situation, the President might be conferring with Cabinet members who could offer little help, while his military advisors in the Cabinet were, by their absence unable to provide the counsel and information needed. Additionally, it was decided that greater unity of effort had to be established within the U.S. Armed Services. The disputing uniformed services that existed in 1941 would have to be unified under a single department.

Reorganization occurred, and in foreign affairs, the functions of the Cabinet were reassigned to a national security forum. It gave the President a small group of advisors who could quickly provide relevant information and advice about foreign threats and crises. During the forty-five years of the Cold War, the National Security Council was called into action many times, and generally it served the American people and their leaders well. The nation's Commander-in-Chief could discuss a crisis with the Director of Central Intelligence, an officer who was not in the Cabinet but who was an important, informed figure in U.S. foreign affairs. The Chairman of the Joint Chiefs of Staff was also a designated member of the National Security Council. As it evolved, the Council became an independent group in government that was alerted when a crisis was so serious that special measures seemed warranted. It was not used as a day-to-day organization. Although it had a staff that coordinated an endless mass of papers, the Council with the

President actively functioning at its leader was a preplanned emergency organization. If it had to be renamed today, it might be called the nation's crisis action team.

Why did the Cabinet prove inadequate in dealing with the crises during World War II and the dangerous years that followed? Perhaps the answer to that question was formulated six years before the Japanese attack on Pearl Harbor. A British officer, Major General J.F.C. Fuller noted that a large, well established organization ultimately falls into method and routine. The inexorable purpose of bureaucracy is to ensure mistakes of the past are never repeated. By refining the day-to-day transactions concerning mistakes, the human element is ultimately removed. Such bureaucratic organizations can become highly efficient—for normal affairs and for routine business. However, they are all but helpless when confronted with an unusual, fast breaking situation that demands action.

In 1864, Lieutenant General Ulysses Simpson Grant, the victor at Vicksburg, took command of the federal army that had been losing battles for the Union. Grant gathered a staff of only fourteen officers to manage the world's largest army. He gave his commanders in the field broad guidance, moved his small staff out of Washington, and left behind a large headquarters that dealt with the routine affairs of administering and supplying the large, dispersed army. Not asking the general what his plans were, President Abraham Lincoln handed the fate of the United States to his chosen military leader and watched. Grant moved with the Army of the Potomac. He directly supervised and personally dealt with the real crisis for the American union: General Robert E. Lee and the Confederate Army of Northern Virginia.[10] Grant's crisis action team worked when several other generals had failed to achieve victory.

After World War II, national security reforms accomplished little more than what Grant had accomplished almost one hundred years previously. A leader with a small, independent staff focused on and managed crises while the general bureaucracy managed day-to-day, routine operations. After a difficult start in the Korean War, national security functioned quite well under President Eisenhower. The former general provided more than seven years of peace and relative prosperity, the most tranquil and prosperous period of the Cold War.

When John F. Kennedy was confronted by his first serious foreign affairs test—The Bay of Pigs—the young leader chose to ignore the often-tested federal group structure for dealing with critical international events. He did not call a meeting of the National Security Council to consider the plans or briefings of the Central Intelligence Agency, schemes to land a band of Cubans on the island to challenge and overthrow Fidel Castro. Kennedy consulted with an ad hoc and constantly changing group of advisors and speech writers. Major figures in the group—Secretary of Defense Robert McNamara, Secretary of State Dean Rusk, and Director of Central Intelligence Allen Dulles—had only recently become acquainted. Witnesses later stated that few members of the group questioned CIA briefs and that White House sessions were dominated by senior officials striving to form initial relationships with one another. The immediate crisis—the invasion of Cuba—appeared to be of secondary concern.[11]

John Kennedy's next Cold War brinksmanship resulted in a better outcome than that of the Bay of Pigs. The Cuban Missile Crisis of 1962 ended when Moscow removed its intermediate range missiles and nuclear warheads from the island after threats from Washington. Again, Kennedy used an ad hoc group including his speech writers, but the group was functional; it included the nation's military leadership and this time, the national security bureaucracy was involved. After the crisis, this group, perhaps in response to earlier criticisms that the President had not used appropriate advisors in the government, was named EXCOM (Executive Committee of the National Security Council). Thirty years later, a number of questions were asked about the American performance during the Cuban missile crisis. The Kennedy Administration's assertion that the world had been spared a nuclear war and that victory had been achieved was questioned. The Soviet Ambassador to Cuba, Alexander Alexeev, stated that.Premier Nikita Khrushchev's announced aim in moving the missiles to Cuba was to ensure that the island would be invaded by the United States.   Since an American assurance that no invasion would occur became part of the bargain with the Soviets to remove their missiles, perhaps the real "winner" was Moscow after all. Then too, President Kennedy's CIA advisor, Ray S. Cline, stated there was no real crisis. The long time and well respected U.S. intelligence officer predicted that there was less than a one-thousand-to-one chance nuclear war would have begun. At the time, the U.S.   had a four-to-one advantage in intercontinental ballistic missiles, overwhelming superiority in bombers, and an eight-to-one edge in nuclear weapons.[12] However, Kennedy's management of the Cuban missile crisis is still considered a brilliant American success. Appearances can in some cases be more important than reality in the management of critical incidents.

Subsequent American presidents returned to Eisenhower's way of dealing with foreign crises through a national security council. During the Gulf of Tonkin Incident and the Vietnam War, the council was of little use. The war was neither sudden or unexpected, and American involvement in the conflict occurred over a number of years with several administrations and was mostly the result of day-to-day deliberations and actions of the U.S. Government. *Bureaucracy Does Its Thing,*[13] a good analysis of America's role in the war, was written by an insider, Robert W. Komer.

Soon after taking office, President Jimmy Carter announced that he would deemphasize his and the National Security Council's participation in foreign affairs and would strengthen the role of the Cabinet.[14] The former Governor of Georgia could refer to his solid achievement in reaching an agreement between Israel and Egypt. However, like Kennedy, Carter, a micro-manager, did not direct national security very well between 1976 and 1980.

4

MATRIX MANAGEMENT

In the 1960s when the U.S. and the Soviet Union were in a serious and expensive race to space, American aerospace firms began organizing themselves to ensure their products would work and would be produced on time. An intervention team, independent from the normal bureaucracy, had the authority to consult with the company's executives, identify a problem developing within a low-level organization or shop, and take corrective action. These companies subjected themselves to two bosses, the normal vertical chain of authority and a new highly authoritative team that had horizontal access to everyone. The functioning of this latter team came to be called matrix management.[15]

Figure 1 depicts simplified matrix management. Although the normal structure of a business displayed by the block diagram at the right is functioning, so too is the intervention unit or critical incident management team shown as Block 2. Like the normal control element represented under Block 1, all the members of the unit in Block 2 have the authority to reach into the structure under Block 1 at any level to give orders or make changes. Normally, people who have never consciously considered matrix management at their places of work are unprepared to consider it. How, one might ask, can a person work for two bosses? The answer is: most people actually have many bosses. Most Americans who have had a typical upbringing in a family have had to answer to both a mother and a father (two bosses) during almost one-third of their lives. Few people have worked for any great length of time without becoming involved in a complex structure of rival authority figures. In the world of American business or government, matrix management is not an unusual arrangement.

Figure 2 represents a critical incident or crisis action arrangement at a corporation or a Fortune 500 company that took the trouble to incorporate a crisis action plan into its operation. The shaded blocks of the ordinary structure at the right denote the corporate officers who have left their day-to-day duties to serve in a designated capacity on the crisis action team. Their crisis plan specifies that team members will not directly intervene in the normal functioning of the company at levels below the first tier of authority.

Consequently, a complete matrix management model has not been accepted in this company, as it has not been in many American corporations. For those officers who have vacated their usual positions to deal with critical situations, it is usually advisable to appoint temporary replacements like deputies or assistants. However, Steven Fink's mid-1980s

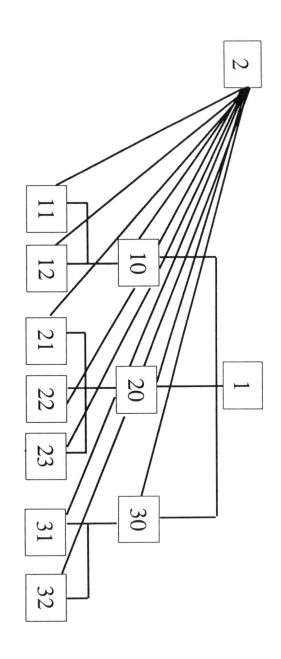

Figure 1: Simplified Matrix Management Model

poll of Fortune 500 companies indicated the median length of an acute crisis situation was approximately two months.[16] When directors are temporarily functioning as members of a crisis action team, their former positions must be filled for the duration of a crisis. The CEO's position might be temporarily filled by one of the company's regional managers. Replacements must be found to cover the jobs of the directors of security, operations and finance. A legal assistant from company headquarters might take the legal counsel's position.

This type of emergency organization—a modified and simplified matrix management model—is neither new nor untried. It forms the basic crisis management for any number of American corporations because of the advantages it offers. One structure performs the essential day-to-day activities of the company without taking responsibility to solve the critical situation that has arisen. This day-to-day structure must respond to the crisis action team whenever it is called upon to do so. In a sense, people are really not working for two bosses. If a crisis is serious, the CEO will probably lead the crisis action team and will also be directing the changes that must be made in company operations. In reality, there is only one boss and the crisis action team members, who are familiar with each other, are assisting the boss in handling a threatening condition. This kind of emergency organization allows a company's best talent to address a special situation without being involved in normal operations. Those people temporarily elevated to manage the company's usual operations are unlikely to try any radical innovations, because when the crisis is past, they will return to their former jobs.

Matrix management is little different than the management the U.S. Government has used in many situations. It worked well for General Grant and President Eisenhower as well as for a number of the country's chief executives. There are enough failures of ad hoc management to warrant a flat assertion that a preplanned response is probably superior to

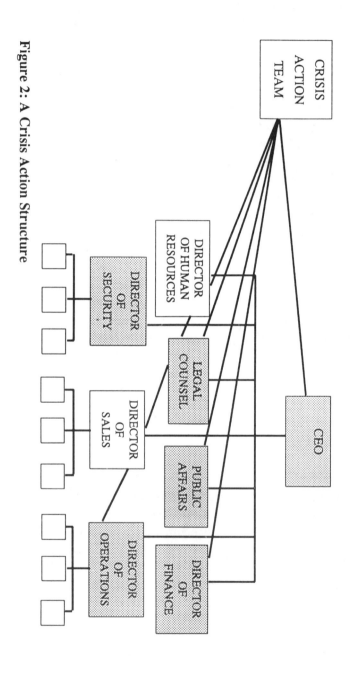

Figure 2: A Crisis Action Structure

waiting for a critical incident to occur and then organizing to confront the situation. Simple common sense indicates that it is better to organize before a crisis occurs than to attempt to organize as the crisis is happening. There is one caution about organization that should be kept in mind. Roger Hilsman, a former Kennedy Administration official and a veteran of several international crises during the early 1960s, was approached by someone advocating a reorganization of the U.S. government's foreign affairs. Hilsman thought and then said, "I am skeptical of organizational gimmicks...the way you improve foreign policy is to get good people into key positions."[17] If a person is not competent, it does not much matter where that person is placed in an organization. Organization is important, but it has limits.

5

LEADERSHIP AND DECISION-MAKING

$\mathbf{F}$ew factors influence the destiny of an organization in crisis more than the leader's initial attitude and the way decisions are reached. Some, to their everlasting regret, have steadily attempted to deny a crisis existed. Others have become so involved in resolving a crisis that they think of little else, adding to their own peril. Any organization will reflect the style of its top management, and it is vitally important to plan for initial success.

In the early 1980s, Johnson & Johnson learned that someone in Chicago was removing packages of the company's Extra-Strength Tylenol pain killer from store shelves. Packages were replaced on shelves but contained some capsules filled with cyanide. Seven unsuspecting customers were soon dead. As the incidents unfolded, there was initially no evidence that Tylenol was directly linked to the deaths. Johnson & Johnson had no crisis management plan, and a considerable amount of time was wasted getting organized to identify and locate experts who could help the company and determine what was happening. (The company now has a crisis management plan; each key member has a copy of it at the office and at home.) During the early crisis incidents, the company's CEO appointed a senior corporate officer to quickly form a seven-man team. It made an early determination to conduct an investigation and to make decisions publicly with consumer interest as a high priority. With diligent work, the team and law enforcement officials soon determined that the product was not being contaminated at the manufacturing site. There was good reason to believe the company was not at fault. Whoever the murderer or murderers were, they were most likely introducing the poison in retail stores, beyond the company's control.

The company's crisis team met twice daily, spent much time traveling and talking to anyone who could produce relevant information. The team was very open and frank with the press. A decision was made to remove Tylenol from stores throughout the country in spite of the belief that contaminated capsules would be found only in Chicago. A considerable amount of money was quickly spent to develop tamper-proof packaging. An expensive public information campaign was begun to inform the world that Tylenol would be back in stores as soon as safe packaging could be manufactured. The company was under pressure from the Director of the Federal Bureau of Investigation, William Webster, who suggested that the product be permanently discontinued because of possible copy-cat cases with other products. The company decided to veto Webster's suggestion. Not long after the headache remedy was reintroduced in new packaging, the product regained most of its market share. Later, a copy-cat tampering incident cost the company once again, but as a result of its management, Johnson & Johnson had earned an enviable reputation. As news stories unfolded, the company was portrayed as a victimized group of concerned, bright, and energetic people who were dedicated to their company's customers.[18]

The management style adopted by Johnson & Johnson leaders successfully avoided a potentially ruinous event. John A. Norris, then the deputy commissioner of the Federal Food and Drug Administration, had carefully observed corporate leadership and defined its management style as "enlightened self-interest." Johnson & Johnson had been determined to end its crisis with its financial health intact. However, the company's top management realized that they also had to recover and maintain public confidence, and achieving that goal would cost money. It must have been tempting to remove Tylenol only from stores in Chicago and inform the public of their success. Much less money would have been lost—at first. However, the product would have been stigmatized. Tylenol, all of it, had to be repackaged so the public could see the newly protected product. In effect, Johnson & Johnson decided to invest in its own future. The investment was sound. Marion K. Pinsdorf, a long time observer of and participant in the business world, advocates a management style that might best be expressed as an attitude. Pinsdorf proposes that an institution consider itself as only a temporary holder of a public franchise.[19] That outlook could be described as "enlightened self-interest." Leaders in both business and government might consider adopting that attitude.

Just as management styles are established by a leader, so too are decision-making styles. Steven Fink identified five types of high pressure decision-making, one effective and four that are ineffective.

Vigilance: The recommended type of crisis and critical incident decision-making, this style features an objective collection of information and focuses attention on the facts. A good example of this kind of decision-making is provided in the Tylenol case. A tremendous amount of effort was put into identifying the particulars so that actions could be based on factual information. The hastily assembled crisis action team was small enough so that internal coordination was kept at a minimum. At the very outset of the incident, the CEO appointed the responsible officer with the simple but unmistakable directive: "Take charge." The CEO then watched, listened, and usually backed up his man with approval, authority, and funds.

Unconflicted Inertia: This type of maladaptive, high pressure decision-making begins with a determination that nothing is going to change. From the start, the overriding feature is that the problem will go away if only it is placed in the right context. The decision-maker's role becomes one of keeping his subordinates' eyes "on the ball," the important issues. The problem is to be reduced in magnitude by the realization that other factors are of greater significance. The quintessential role model for unconflicted inertia is President Richard M. Nixon during the Watergate scandal. Nixon's decision not to make changes when the facts began to emerge cost him dearly. The truth of the case will probably never be fully known, but there is much evidence pointing to a conclusion that the President was not fully aware of all the sophomoric shenanigans of his henchmen. Nixon had the opportunity to conduct his own investigation, make public his findings, and fire subordinates. Instead, Nixon decided to weather "the growing cancer on the Presidency," a "cancer" that eventually destroyed him. By initially choosing this type of decision-making, the leader sends a message that the course has already been plotted. Subordinates are understandably reluctant to offer an alternative path. There appears to be no need for the "devil's advocate," a subordinate who questions the majority view and points out weaknesses in the option being selected. Robert F. Kennedy cited the lack of a devil's advocate as one of the prime failures in the decision-making leading to the Bay of Pigs debacle.

Unconflicted Change: Here is the leader whose thinking and actions are heavily influenced by the advice he last heard. The decision process seems to have no guiding principles, no end goal. The leader will appear as a person of indecision, one who will change course with little warning. What is lacking is the all important quality of consistency. At the very least, this type of decision- making fails to attract trust. In business, no one wants to become a partner with an organization or manager that decides only to then change the decision without apparent reason. In public service, voters are unlikely to support a new candidate, because they are uncertain about the consequences of their choice. The example in this case is Walter Mondale's 1984 vacillation over his choice for a campaign manager to head up his run for the presidency. In just a few days, Mondale switched his views three times. On each occasion, he was apparently being influenced by successive news accounts in the press. While he was demonstrating an inability to decide, the voters evidently had little trouble in making their own choice. The reelection of President Ronald Reagan was one of the most overwhelming statements of presidential preference the American people have ever made.

Defensive Avoidance: Closely akin to unconflicted inertia, this style of decision-making is marked by laying blame at the doorstep of others as well as maybe even denying a problem exists. In both types of decision processes, the leader is likely to "stonewall" the press, dodging questions or refusing to become available for interviews. Both cases may also be marked by the "cover up," the deliberate attempt to suppress information that might be damaging to the decision-maker. The difference is that in defensive avoidance, the fact that a problem exists may sometimes be acknowledged. It is just that the problem will be made out to be of someone else's making, or it might be wholly charged to a natural occurrence. In 1979, Metropolitan Edison, the operating company at the Three Mile Island nuclear power plant, initially denied there was anything wrong at the site. Most observers charged the corporate leadership with attempting a "cover-up." Another example might be the A.H. Robbins Company in its handling of controversy surrounding its intrauterine device, the Dalkon Shield. There was evidence linking the product to the deaths of twenty-one women and charges that the company was suppressing damaging data. In the end, in 1985, the $11 million profit from the sales of the devices was dwarfed by $375 million in damage payments and $107 million in legal fees.

Hyper -Viglilance: This type of high pressure decision-making blocks out all but the immediate problem. Other duties and normal operations are shirked in a totally focused effort to resolve the incident. While some other styles work to deny there is a problem, this style denies there is anything except the problem. An appropriate example of this kind of maladaptive decision-making was vividly demonstrated by President Carter during the Iranian Hostage Crisis of 1980. After the failure of the April rescue attempt, the President largely confined himself to the White House grounds and focused on the hostage problem. The author of this book, as the commander of the rescue element, Delta Force, could easily see there was precious little chance of attempting another raid, because security surrounding the captive Americans had been so tightened that a second try would not only have been suicidal, it would have probably resulted in many deaths among those who were to have been rescued. The diplomatic overture was being handled through the offices of the Algerian Government so there appeared to be little the President could do. Yet Carter refused to devote much attention to the nation's many other problems and tried to give the impression he simply had no time for political campaigning against his challenger, Ronald Reagan. Whether President Carter's actions were merely a ploy to gain voter sympathy or an indication of actual conditions, they were ruinous to his administration. Carter's actions were much on the mind of President George Bush during his own decision-making period in the late summer and fall of 1990, a time when he was deciding whether or not to go to war in the Persian Gulf. Despite a flurry of media criticism, Bush refused to interrupt his vacation, handled problems other than Iraq's invasion of Kuwait, and proceeded with studied deliberation. The contrast with Carter's behavior could not have been more stark.[20]

More than initial attitude and decision-making style affect the overall impact a leader makes in dealing with a sudden crisis. One of the nation's recognized experts on the art of leadership, Perry M. Smith, claims that a leader has a responsibility to train subordinates for a crisis situation. Unless a chief executive officer trains people, they will not know the leader's standards and expectations when a crisis occurs. If subordinates are unrehearsed and uninformed, they should not later bear the burden of failure by themselves. Additionally, when a leader describes the solution of a crisis before examining all of the facts in the situation, that leader is telling subordinates that no one needs to be bothered with alternatives. Everyone in the crisis is consequently taking a particularly dangerous course. Before his assassination, Robert F. Kennedy made a special point of outlining the dangers of subordinates telling a leader only what they think the leader wants to hear. A healthy atmosphere in a business or a public office permits a frank discussion of the unpleasant and the unpopular. If a leader establishes the right atmosphere, everyone's opinion should merit respect and a fair hearing before a decision is made. Intellectual worth should not be confused with rank or standing. However, the leader must establish a practical balance. When immediate action is needed to overcome a serious threat, an immediate solution may be far superior to the "best" solution, a course that may be contingent on surviving the crisis for a long period of time.[21]

Finally, leadership does not include only logic or experience. Some leaders have a quality that cannot be taught or instilled. It is prescience, an ability to become aware of trouble before it occurs, or to formulate solutions before they are evident to others. The person who has this gift is apt to succeed and prevail in very different situations. In 1985, The Home State Savings Bank Case, as it became known, involved the potential collapse in Ohio of seventy financial institutions that operated without federal deposit insurance. When banks are placed in jeopardy, panic can cause a self-fulfilling prophecy. Depositors, thinking the banks might fail, withdraw their accounts and thereby cause failure. Good crisis management in these difficult situations involved accurate, timely information as to what assets the banks actually possessed.

When the Home State Savings Bank Case started to unfold, Karen Horn, President of the Federal Reserve Bank in Cleveland, immediately determined that radical action was warranted. She could have tried to avoid the situation by treating it as a state, not a federal problem. Initially she only had hints and rumors about the banks, and this information did not seem serious. Horn followed her instincts, disregarded standard practices and regulations, and quickly assembled every bank examiner she could find. She rented a fleet of telephone-equipped Lincoln Continentals and dispatched her investigators throughout the state. Within a short time, the magnitude of the problem was known. In possession of the facts, the governor of the state and federal and state bank officials could make decisions with some confidence. A potential disaster was averted.[22]

Leadership is a highly personalized skill. Each person will use it differently, and although some behavior patterns can be changed or modified, people are not apt to successfully make extensive changes in their own character. However, it is important for a leader to set the tone and attitude, because they will be reflected in everyone's behavior. A vigilant and open approach to a serious problem, not an obsessive or secretive approach, is recommended. Leaders must train subordinates for crises or live with what happens when those crises arrive. Leaders must also establish an atmosphere that breeds consultations of candor and honesty. They should consciously avoid situations in which subordinates are telling their chief what they believe their leader wants to hear. In stressful circumstances, a quick reaction is often not the "best" action, but a leader should often try to quickly avoid a dangerous situation, rather than strive for a painfully distant solution to the same situation. It must, however, be acknowledged that luck and inexplicable personal characteristics are an important part of leadership. Leaders can be trained, but many good ones were apparently born to lead.

6

USING
EXPERTS
AND
CONSULTANTS

As a general principle, it is a good idea to obtain independent opinions. However, in the midst of a critical incident, getting opinions should never be automatic. Using experts can be dangerous at a stressful time and in an on-going crisis. Finding a useful consultant can be time-consuming, and time is usually a vital commodity. In some instances, there is not much choice, particularly when a leader is dealing with an unfamiliar environment, one that is not fully understood but is well known to others. Generally, a leader should identify in advance the expertise to be needed. Often a leader should become acquainted with

experts to become familiar with their thinking to use their
services later, when the leader's institution is threatened.

At a critical moment during the Vietnam War, President
Lyndon B. Johnson asked for advice from a group of
distinguished advisors after the devastating Communist Tet
Offensive in January 1968. Although the North Vietnamese
and their Viet Cong allies suffered great losses, previous
American statements about South Vietnam's cities being safe
had proved embarrassing. Supposedly winning the war, U.S.
and South Vietnamese soldiers had suddenly found
themselves fighting for their lives in cities. Knowing the
press had emphasized the great losses in the offensive,
Johnson met with some of the nation's most distinguished
former soldiers and diplomats, including General Matthew
B. Ridgway, General Maxwell Taylor, as well as Clark
Clifford and George Ball. Soon named by the press as the
"wise men," the group listened to briefings on the war and
offered the President their advice and counsel.

The President was surprised at the group's
recommendations. They had concluded the United States
was losing the war and should withdraw. Johnson could not
keep their conclusions to himself, reasoning that the men
could easily go to the press and make their views known.
The President would then find himself on the defensive,
publicly arguing with his own chosen advisors. Angrily,
Johnson recalled the people who had briefed the group and
demanded to know "who poisoned the well." Hearing what
his group of experts had previously heard, the President
concluded there was nothing wrong with the briefings. The
"wise men" had evidently reached their conclusions before
the briefings or had only heard what they wanted to hear.
Shortly thereafter, Johnson announced his decision not to run
for a second term in office, thereby avoiding the decision to
begin America's negotiated withdrawal from the war in
Southeast Asia.[23]

Johnson's "wise men" were so prominent that they could not be ignored or dismissed. Their wisdom and advice could not be simply overlooked. Their conclusions had to be carefully weighed and considered. In business, leaders should be cautious about calling on former CEOs or well-known figures in the business for advice. The experts might have their own agenda.

Finding the useful consultant can take time. During the 1985 Home State Savings Bank Case, the Governor of Ohio, Richard Celeste, spent an entire day trying to find a disinterested expert on savings banks to act as an advisor and assistant. Celeste was successful and hired a man he did not know, an acquaintance of the governor's own father. The governor and his aides had less than two weeks to resolve the bank crisis, and one has to wonder why the State Government of Ohio could not produce adequate expertise from its own membership or from federal resources.[24]

Time can be saved if a company or a government office maintains a list of trusted advisors who periodically render services. Any enterprise or administration is apt to find itself in unfamiliar situations, and leaders will need advice about them. Retirees can often provide experience and expertise, and paying for a few days of their time each year can be a wise investment. Additionally, leaders should listen to these outsiders in order to detect any biases, flaws or particular strengths. In business, most large companies—about seventy percent of the Fortune 500—plan to use outside consultants in times of crisis.[25]

For businesses there is a special, growing need for expertise in overseas, foreign environments. Because of the steady growth in international trade, American companies that sell products abroad often find themselves dependent on off-shore resources. They can become vulnerable—without knowing it. Typical risks businesses face involve changes in a regime, political turmoil, third party intervention, and revisions in governmental policies. All of these risks can drive an unsuspecting corporation into financial turmoil within hours. A company may find itself very dependent on one of the "old hands" the company may have used to facilitate its operations in a foreign land. If a corporation requires the help of foreign consultants, they should be well known to the corporation before being employed. CEOs should get to know their emergency consultants before emergencies occur.[26]

There is some merit in having an outside consultant examine emergency procedures and plans, but for some well defined areas, consultants are of little use. Unless a specific weakness exists, a successful CEO probably has little use for advisors on day-to-day operations. After all, the CEO is the veteran who should be knowledgeable. Corporation officers should be particularly wary of advice from outside people, who in their own field of expertise, have no experience in manufacturing, distribution, sales, or service. Holders of political office should be skeptical of advice from consultants who claim to know constituents' needs but have never themselves run for office. Successful vote getters would do well to trust their instincts about public needs and popular attitudes. One should evaluate ignorance and inexperience before assembling a list of consultants.

Whether advisors and consultants are helpful or harmful largely depends on the care and consideration that were given to their appointments. Politicians and people in businesses want the best counsel and advice available, but having a famous advisor can be risky. In a crisis in a foreign country an ambassador or police leader may be necessary, and a CEO must be familiar with their capabilities and limitations before they are asked to help. Above all, outsider consultants are only useful in providing advice about what needs to be known. They should never be hired for their knowledge about something already known.

7

A
CRISIS
ACTION
PLAN

Evidence exists that organizations with an emergency plan do better in a crisis than organizations without such plans. Steven Fink's famous survey during the 1980s produced an important distinction between those companies with a crisis management plan and those without one. When a crisis did occur, the companies without these plans endured their difficulties two-and-a-half times longer than those organizations with plans. Fink's survey might have simply divided the prudent companies from the less well managed organizations.[27]

The best plans are short, well understood by participants, and flexible enough to accommodate unanticipated contingencies. There should be no mystery about a plan, nor should there be any great faith placed in it. The chief advantage of tackling troubles with a plan, instead of relying on an ad hoc response, is that time is saved in having gotten organized. A plan is not likely to solve a problem—only people can do that. A good plan simply ensures that appropriate attention is given to a problem and that decision-makers can take quick action, devoting a minimum amount of their time to other matters. There is no reason to create a special critical incident plan, if an adequate crisis management plan already exists. The two cases are similar. The crisis management plan should adequately deal with critical incidents.

A good plan answers the questions: who, what, when, where, why, and how? Corporate and government plans may be similar, differing only in focus. Government plans often focus upon the public safety of lives and property. Public safety is, of course, a prime reason for the existence of government itself. A major concern of governmental plans involves how and under what circumstances should the public be informed, warned, or both. A good civic plan takes into consideration extreme conditions like an approaching hurricane or a predictable earthquake when power, broadcast, and telephone service are interrupted and a door-to-door notification procedure is necessary.[28] Corporate emergency plans are often focused upon the survival of the company, but the best corporate plans take into account the interests of the public. Good corporate plans are written to complement civic plans, especially in cases of natural disasters and threats to the environment like air pollution or gas pipe leaks.

What follows is a fictional crisis action plan which will be examined in detail. The company, "Jet Oil," is fictional and any similarity between it and an actual company, either existing or previously existing, is purely coincidental.

Jet Oil Crisis Management Plan
(with Commentaries)

This plan is to be executed at the direction of the CEO or by a corporate officer designated or approved by the CEO. The plan is intended to resolve a serious problem in the day-to-day operations of the company, placing deliberation, planning, and action in the hands of the fewest number of essential, key personnel who can initiate quick, coordinated, and effective action. It is appropriate to activate this plan on report of:

1. a major oil spill involving the company.
2. a major fire on company property.
3. a sudden shortage of product.
4. an incident on company property involving loss of life.
5. an incident of terrorism.
6. an act of God severe enough to jeopardize company operations.
7. an event of similar seriousness to the above.

Comment: This part of the plan answers the questions: why and when? Note that the CEO is personally holding the decision to form the crisis management team. Others can recommend, but the CEO is the only one to decide on forming the team. Although having one person responsible for forming a team seems restrictive, keep in mind that many American companies have considerable turbulence in their executive offices. In a two year period during the mid-1980s, forty-one percent of the financial officers, twenty-seven percent of the human resources officers, and twenty-four percent of the CEO's of America's Fortune 500 companies were replaced.[29] Limiting the formation of the team to one person, however, is not good practice in government. A previously designated transfer of authority should be stated in case principal leaders are incapacitated or unable to effect control. In government, there should always be some designated residual authority and capability to protect lives and property, although that authority and capability may come from neighboring or higher jurisdictions.

It should be noted that the company is anticipating some definite kinds of critical incidents or crises. In the last category, the reference to "an event of similar seriousness" is made to cover any contingency.

When the CEO declares the need for crisis action, the Director of Operations will place the twenty-four hour duty officer on duty and initiate a telephone watch and crisis log in the Operations Center. The Director of Operations will clear the Operations Center Conference Room for the use of the Crisis Action Team and will also recommend to the CEO any appropriate additions to the Jet Oil Crisis Action Team.

Comment: This section has answered the question: where? Also, it has established a round-the-clock situation room, a meeting place, and a log of events. The operations section of the company was probably selected as a site, because it would likely have the best communications and would be in contact with all the company's facilities on a day-to-day basis. It is prudent to remember that the log, a useful tool to collect and disseminate information, may be used in a court room in the event of a sizeable catastrophe or in serious litigation. It may become an important document, subject to subpoena.

The Jet Oil Crisis Action Team is headed by the CEO and includes the Director of Operations, the Corporate Legal Officer, the Director of Public Relations, the Director of Security, and other team members designated by the CEO.

Team members or consultants may be hired from outside the company if needed during the crisis. **Comment:** This part of the plan answers the question: who? It is an important and vital part of the plan, because it is simple human nature to avoid unpleasant duties or shun an event that might later reflect unfavorably on participants. Emergency action responsibilities should be written into job descriptions, and officers should be counseled on their performances under stress. There should be no question as to whom is expected to do what. The number of members is probably at the absolute minimum and might have to be augmented as suggested in the plan. Depending on the size of the company, a weakness may exist in this plan, because it does not indicate who will be temporarily designated to assume the principal officers' positions during their absence. In a small company, a small number of team members might be normal and necessary. In a large corporation, temporary replacements should be designated for members of the Crisis Action Team.

The Director of Operations is responsible for providing the Operations Center Conference Room with appropriate information, telephone-number lists, maps, research and the crisis log book. The Director of Operations will recommend to the CEO a daily meeting time for all members of the Crisis Action Team and is responsible for informing team members of the meeting time. He may assemble members of the team without the presence of the CEO at anytime. The Director of Operations will act in the company's best interest during the CEO's absence and if the CEO is out of communications, the Director of Operations may publicly represent the CEO's views.

All members of the team are expected to inform themselves on the nature of the crisis and be prepared to recommend actions and solutions to the CEO. All members of the team must not think in terms of their designated corporate position, but must think about what is best for the company, anticipate problems, and recommend actions that will lead to the best possible outcome for the company.

Comment: This section answers the question: how? The Jet Oil Crisis Action Team will function, because all members are responsible for informing themselves about what is happening. Assigning responsibility to everyone alleviates a common situation in which some team members might avoid responsibility, claiming they were not aware of a particular circumstance. Clearly, team members must phone the duty officer to keep themselves up-to-date on log entries. If they did not, the Director of Operations would be required to spend a great deal of time finding other team members to keep them informed. Note also that although the Jet Oil CEO reserved the right to form the team, once the plan is implemented, the CEO recognizes the need for quick decisions and has authorized the Director of Operations to act in the CEO's absence. Additionally, the CEO wants team members to see beyond their specialties and to think and act as company leaders would during difficult times. When a situation becomes tense, the CEO does not want to waste time as a referee for internal disputes that are bound to occur because of natural, divided responsibilities and outlooks. Note also the plan suggests a possible general goal: the best possible outcome for the company.

Members of the Crisis Action Team will keep themselves fully informed of the current corporate position concerning the critical incident or crisis. Every team member will be prepared to meet with media representatives at any time and represent the company's views. It is company policy that rumors and false stories must be dispelled and denied at the earliest opportunity and that the company side of an issue must be put forward as early and as often as possible. **Comment:** The last part of the plan is controversial. Most corporate and public sector emergency plans designate only one company spokesperson with the idea that consistency is the supreme consideration. Here, the emphasis is on aggressiveness, speed, and the ability to represent the company from several locations simultaneously, an important consideration for an oil company.

No matter how complete and brilliantly composed, plans are only as good as they are understood and executed. The Jet Oil Crisis Management Plan is short in length, but it answers the basic questions: who, what, why, where, when and how. The best plans are written, coordinated, and revised by those people who must use them. Occasionally, plans should be used just to ensure that primary people remain up-to-date on the contents and procedures. Plans do not cover all contingencies, but an organization is better with a plan prepared for emergencies than attempting to improvise one in the midst of a fast moving, threatening situation.

8

CONFRONTING THE NEWS MEDIA

It is powerful. Most people are familiar with it but do not understand it. They feel helpless in the face of it but rarely realize they can affect it. It is the news media.

Most agree on the power of news media, and that power is usually referred to regretfully. In evaluating the negative effects of previous crises, thirty-two percent of the respondents in Fink's Fortune 500 poll cited close government scrutiny. Fifty-five percent of the victims cited bad times interfering with business, and fifty-two percent cited lasting financial woes. Another thirty-five percent cited a damaged corporate image. However, the most frequent negative effect, claimed by seventy-two percent, was media scrutiny.[30] In almost all of these cases, media attention portrayed a reversal of good fortune for the corporations. When a company is in crisis, the price of its stock is likely to fall. If the beleaguered corporation is privately owned, customers may lose confidence in it and seek to do business with competitors. For most businesses, attention from print and broadcast media can occasionally be helpful, but media scrutiny is mostly associated with scandal, consumer fraud, or defective products. Enough media scrutiny can cause devastating results.

The public official in government perceives the news media differently. Michael Blumenthal, a high ranking official in both industry and government during the 1970s, compared the two worlds. He concluded that while the criterion for success in business was the bottom line; in public life, the deciding factor was the appearance of success.[31] His view, perhaps an accurate one, holds that a president, governor, or mayor does not have to actually do anything about public debt, for example; the official only has to give the appearance of working on the problem of indebtedness. The news media often equates image with substance. Some successful politicians are fond of saying that mere presence is eighty percent of their jobs.

Few public crises more vividly demonstrated the difference between fact and appearance in the media than the case of the *S.S. Mayaguez*. With the evacuation of the American Embassy in Cambodia and the triumph of the brutal Khmer Rouge in that country during the spring of 1975, the fortunes of President Gerald Ford appeared dim. The United States seemed to be in retreat and to have lost confidence. When the communists seized the American container ship, the *S.S. Mayaguez* and its crew off the coast of Cambodia, it looked as if Washington was not simply being driven from Southeast Asia; America was to be humiliated. Ford called

the National Security Council into session and determined to
use immediate action to recover the ship and crew.

Twenty-three U.S. airmen, attempting to join rescue forces,
were killed in an accident during a hurried helicopter flight
in nearby Thailand. Marines failed to land where the crew of
the *S.S. Mayaguez* was being detained. They did land on a
heavily fortified, communist-held island where they rapidly
found themselves in serious combat. Fifteen Marines were
killed; fifty were wounded; and three were reported missing
in action. Meanwhile, the ship's captain and crew had been
freed and were enroute to their ship. In the U.S., President
Ford's public approval rating rose from thirty-nine percent to
fifty-one percent. What turned a very dubious performance
into a minor triumph was the way it was presented in the
American news media. The President was portrayed as being
decisive, and the United States appeared resolute after a
period   of   demonstrated   helplessness.   Appearance,
perception, and image had overshadowed the facts.[32]

Although public officials in government must gain
approval and success in the news media, business people
often shun press and broadcast reporters. Increasingly, the
news media is being regarded with fear and loathing. During
the late 1970s and early 1980s, approval of the news media
steadily declined in national polls. Some of the drop in
public esteem was self-inflicted. Janet Cooke, a Washington
Post reporter, won a Pulitzer Prize for a story that was
revealed later to be pure fiction. Japanese reporters, ignoring
an opportunity to intervene or notify police, elbowed and
fought one another to get an unobstructed view of a murder.
In a 1977 pronouncement, an American television news
executive stated he would not wait one day to broadcast a
story about an American agent, even if the delay might save
the agent's life. The executive feared being scooped by
competitors. Finally, there is the repeated air crash and
disaster scenario for American broadcast media—tight

close-ups of shocked survivors and horrified witnesses; microphones thrust into tearful faces of bereaved relatives; reporters appointing themselves as aviation experts, judges, and people's defenders. They seemed to fault the corporation and seek public esteem for themselves.[33]

Much anger and fear are directed at the television news media, a business that is often misunderstood. It is usually described as a new visual medium. Turning off the audio component of a news program will reveal how much the medium depends on its verbal message. It is informative to compare the front page and editorial page of The New York Times with that day's television network news coverage and commentary. Newspaper people derisively refer to their television counterparts as "rip and read heads," pleasant looking people who are plagiarizing a newspaper reporter's hard earned intellectual property by reading it from a studio teleprompter. Those who decry or attempt to mystify television claim the medium depends on a novel means of communication: the sound bite, the short, highly descriptive but intellectually shallow story. However, most people only read a newspaper's headlines for most stories and editorials, studying in detail only the articles and commentaries that interest them. Newspapers have been communicating via "sound bites" for several centuries. Television just adopted the newspapers' practice.[34] Newspapers also have visual aspects. William Randolph Hearst's oft-quoted dictum to the newspaper artist Frederick Remington—"You supply the pictures, I'll supply the war" —is usually cited as exemplifying yellow, jingoistic journalism. However, the publisher was demanding a visual representation to accompany the stories in his paper. That kind of journalism—the-story-and-picture —had been standard for almost forty years before the Spanish-American War. Television also uses the story and picture, and neither should be feared.

In some cases and for some audiences, a corporation can establish its own media. Johnson & Johnson bought special 800 telephone lines to communicate with anyone, anywhere who wanted to talk about Tylenol or ask questions about its safety. Johnson & Johnson bought television advertisements, full page newspaper ads, magazine space, and a cross country electronic news conference to enlighten the public attitude, to convey its good intentions, and to publicized its new tamper-proof product packaging. Johnson & Johnson answered every one of the thousands of letters it received during the crisis.[35] In a significant way, the company established its own media. The Mobil Corporation provides another example of advocacy advertising and aggressive communication. Given the wherewithal to buy print space, the victimized corporation of a one column reporter's attack can retaliate with an eight column response, often in the same newspaper.

Arguments can be made in favor of shunning any contact with news media during a threatening or embarrassing event. Warren Anderson, the CEO of Union Carbide during the Bhopal crisis, said the company's lawyers would have been happy if he had locked himself in a room and refused to communicate with reporters. Naturally, corporate legal counsel is concerned about statements that might be later used in court by a plaintiff seeking damages from a corporation.[36] If a privately held company is in a crisis but is sure of its customers' good will and continued patronage, there seems little use in subjecting company officers to questions by the press.

Experience with the media does suggest that "no comment" is very risky. During 1978, the Love Canal area in upstate New York was found to be contaminated. Hooker Chemical, a subsidiary of Occidental Petroleum, was charged with causing miscarriages, congenital malformations and the emergency evacuation of 236 families who had built homes on one of Hooker's former dump sites. Occidental's policy was to save its defense for court and avoid or "stonewall" the press. As a result, the fact that Hooker had been forced to sell the land to the local school board under threat of condemnation some twenty years before the evacuation went unreported. That Hooker had informed the local government of the nature of the dump site was unreported. The fact that Hooker recommended against any public use of the site other than for a park site was unreported. That Hooker possessed the local government's signed release from corporate responsibility went unreported and therefore unrevealed to the public. The fact that the degree of pollution and number of damage claims were overstated was not publicized. Meanwhile, Occidental, retaining its policy of silence, saw the price of its stock drop until losses amounted to half a billion dollars.[37] Unfortunately, today, "no comment" is equated with "guilty as charged." Reflecting on his long experience in the automobile manufacturing business, including time as the CEO of American Motors, Gerald C. Meyers concluded that most public relations campaigns are lost through silence because of overly zealous and overly cautious legal advice.[38]

In most cases, there are better arguments for communicating about a crisis than remaining silent. Communicating quickly and fully provides a business with a chance to take the offensive, seize the initiative, and shape the nature of the discussion. It provides the opportunity to become proactive, not simply reactive. It also affords the opportunity to correct erroneous information and dispel rumors. Moreover, refusing to communicate and answer charges can give the impression that an organization is arrogant, uncaring, and contemptuous of the public.[39]

If a business decides to communicate its side of an issue, some important tactics should be considered. If possible, the press conference format should be used rather than the

one-on-one interview. The choice provides the business with
the advantage of selecting its own site and moves cameras
away from a possibly damaging scene. Also, the press
conference permits the representative of the business to
select questioners and to end the session when it seems
advantageous. A press conference allows the business to
chose the time for the meeting. If a conference is held late in
the day, reporters may not have the opportunity to verify
statements or obtain dissenting views, and the company's
version of the story might be aired or printed without
challenge. A Friday night or Saturday release of information
may not attract the attention that a weekday story might. On
weekends, television news crews and newspaper teams are
often composed of different people than the weekday crews.
The timing of press conferences is particularly important
when the price of the company's stock may be affected.
Finally, if a business must make public something that is
potentially embarrassing, it should never schedule that press
conference during the month of August or between
Christmas and New Year's Day. Usually nothing
newsworthy happens in those periods, and a company's
embarrassing news could appear on page one instead of page
twelve.[40]

Almost all of the literature dealing with media relations
stresses the need to have a single spokesperson to ensure
consistency in what the organization wants said. In the event
of a great natural disaster or man-made catastrophe, the
Federal Emergency Management Agency stresses that the
national government must speak with a "consistent and
coordinated voice."[41] The whole thrust of the agency's
public information planning is to represent other federal
entities with its public affairs management. Unfortunately,
the agency is assuming that the news audience is so naive
that differences of opinion or different views of the same set
of facts within an organization are impossible or at least

unlikely. Also, the agency is assuming that reporters in the news media can be controlled to cover a story in only one way.

Reality is different. During the 1990-1991 Persian Gulf War, the U.S. Government emerged as a thoroughly competent, believable organization. Sometimes, however, White House statements were occasionally at odds with statements being made at the Department of Defense. Officers at press briefings were changed repeatedly at the department until Lieutenant General Thomas Kelly, the operations officer of the Joint Chiefs of Staff, came before the cameras. Kelly seemed to exude honesty and was retained as the prime Pentagon spokesman. At the Central Command Headquarters in Saudi Arabia, officers at press briefings were also changed repeatedly during the preparatory stages of the war. Finally, the command selected Marine Brigadier General Richard I. Neal, an officer who had not been trained in public affairs. When the commander, General Norman Schwarzkopf seemed responsible and believable to the American people, he began to represent his own command to reporters. The respect and admiration of the American people for their military forces soared. There never was a single spokesperson for the government, and even at the end of the war, what General Schwarzkoph said sometimes conflicted with pronouncements from the White House. Perhaps some differences seemed to make the U.S. Government's story more credible with the American people. Consistency has value, but a slick, glib spokesperson may be seen as slick and glib, particularly by a people whose resistance to hucksters and sales pitches is second nature to their character.

If no opportunity exists to attract reporters into a news conference, some tactics should be considered in one-on-one media encounters. The first rule is to establish the ground rules. Interviews with reporters can be classified into four categories.

On the Record: Everything can be reported including the name and position of the person being interviewed.

Background: Direct quotes are normally not used unless the interviewer gets consent from the source. The person being interviewed might be identified as "an industry spokesperson," "a knowledgeable official," or "a departmental source."

Deep Background: The person being interviewed is not identified in any way. Information is only to be revealed on consent of the person interviewed. When revealed, information is usually prefaced by "We understand that" or "We have learned that."

Off the Record: The reporter is not to use what is said. However, it might be considered fair for the reporter to mention another situation at another place and time and draw a comparison, a comparison that might lead the reporter to draw a conclusion in concert with what the source revealed.[42]

It should, of course, be kept in mind that some reporters claim journalism is not a profession, and therefore, it has no professional ethics. Despite a widespread popular notion to the contrary, judges can make reporters reveal their sources. Probably, only the cases in which stubborn newspeople refuse to yield information are cited on the nightly news and in the nation's newspapers. A reporter revealing names to a judge might well fail the test of "newsworthiness" at some editor's desk. The best rule for public relations officers is, regardless of the agreed-upon ground rules, nothing should be said that would not have been said "on the record."

General Frederick C. Weyand was one of the few senior military officers to earn a favorable press during the Vietnam

War. He would often begin a press interview with the question, "What's your story line?" Surprisingly, many reporters would repeat instructions their editors had given them or discuss the nature of the story they hoped to report. Informed about what reporters wanted, Weyand would help them realize their goals, always putting a favorable "spin" on any discussion. This initial give-and-take between an interviewer and a press conference leader can reveal a reporter's bias or preconception. It is also helpful to have a fact sheet available so the reporter has information in black and white. Additionally, anyone giving a press briefing should have reporters' phone numbers at home and at work. In the event something occurs that should be revealed, reporters can be immediately contacted.[43]

Leaders may be only one source of the information from the organization for the news media. When a company or government administration is under pressure, most employees see themselves at the center of a crisis, finally anticipating their day of notoriety. Washington *Post* reporters Carl Bernstein and Robert Woodward uncovered the Watergate scandal by interviewing secretaries and guards in the Nixon Administration. Communications between employees and reporters require special consideration and delicate handling. Forbidding employees from speaking to the press not only raises constitutional questions, it is apt to encourage both reporters and employees to suspect all is not well with top management. Leaders in a well managed organization will keep all employees informed and provide up-to-date information, as a critical incident or crisis unfolds. Employees can and should be encouraged to direct media inquiries to the public affairs office, but moves by top management to restrain employees can be counterproductive.

Media should be handled with candor. When the Hygrade Food Products company was faced with a serious product contamination scare in 1982, the Vice President for

Operations, Charles Ledgerwood, was placed in charge of
the crisis management team. Ledgerwood determined he
would be open and honest with the press. Rumors and stories
were spreading that some of the company's Ball Park
frankfurters contained razor blades and nails. The
frankfurters earned almost $160 million in annual sales, a
substantial part of the company's profits. During the crisis,
management feared the entire organization was at risk. The
product was withdrawn and examined. Tests proved the near
impossibility of interjecting metal objects during the
processing of the product. Police began questioning people
claiming they had bought contaminated packages of the
brand. Soon, fourteen claimants admitted to lying in hopes of
getting a monetary settlement. Hygrade had spent $30,000 in
a public relations campaign and lost approximately one
million dollars in sales. However, reporters rallied to the
company's cause and widely publicized the attempted
extortion. The product regained its popularity. Ledgerwood
credited the company's initial openness and candor toward
reporters with the favorable media response when the
attempted extortion became known. Reflecting on the crisis,
Ledgerwood concluded that honesty was helpful. He advised
against yielding to the temptation of writing half-truths in
press releases, because they could lead to being caught in a
web of lies.[44]
    The news media is important but should not be feared.
There is a long history of press and broadcast relations with
organizations, and that experience can be used to coach
management to prepare for moments of trial. There is no
reason to surround television journalism with mystery. The
television journalist may be looking for the "sound bite," but
the print reporter has always been looking for the headline.
The bright, well informed press representative should think
ahead and help reporters get their "sound bites" and
headlines. Nevertheless, it will not be a pleasant encounter.

In America, the news media tends to hold both business and government guilty until proven innocent. However, media representatives, clamoring for answers from a besieged organization need information. Otherwise, they would not bother to attend a press conference. They are seeking the knowledgeable leader, the expert. The job of the leader is to ensure rumors are stopped, false stories are corrected; and the interests of the organization are protected and nurtured. With all that responsibility, the leader must not slight the needs of the organization's people who also have expertise. In speaking to the press, the leader must always remember that honesty is the best policy.

9

MANAGING STRESS OF VICTIMS AND LEADERS IN A CRISIS

During a critical incident or crisis, a leader not only deals with the proximate cause but also deals with effects that often involve people under stress. In a natural or man-made disaster, management duties may involve providing aid and assistance to workers' distraught families or helping suffering workers themselves. Stress can also be produced by people's imperfect knowledge about an organization undergoing difficult times. Of course, stress is not unknown to top management or senior officials.

Often, the people in charge are the least affected by a critical incident. They will be involved and absorbed while the action is occurring. They are not likely to have the time to take account of their emotional feelings. In the midst of rapid, changing situations, fatigue is dangerous. A leader should take breaks, temporarily find a replacement, and go outside. Staying overly long in a fast paced, chaotic environment can lead to a siege mentality when participants begin to feed on their own fears and concerns. Serious effects on leaders usually appear when the crisis has ended. It is then that a period of self-doubt, self-blame, second guessing and guilt begins. A cure for this executive gloom is to hold a post-action decompression session where everyone is given a chance to critique the team's performance and decide on what has to be done to prevent a reoccurrence of the crisis.[45]

In life-threatening events, responsible managers and public officials must be quick to respond to victims as well as to their families. Often, small considerations are initially helpful: providing child care while a wife visits her husband in a hospital, performing essential household errands that might go undone, helping victims financially by paying rent, and notifying relatives to help victims. Consideration must be given to the mental state of people who have experienced horror or performed duties at a disaster. New York's Nassau County law enforcement officers were fortunate to work in a department that had already established a peer-support group when Avianca Flight 052 crashed in 1990. The group, trained to counsel officers involved in traumatic incidents, helped shocked policemen recover from emotional stress after they had removed seventy-three bodies of men, women and children from the wreckage.[46] Peer-support groups are easily arranged and cost little more than forethought and some fundamental instruction. How well an organization weathers a disaster sometimes depends on how well that organization takes care of its own members.

Information and morale are matters of support. In a crisis, employees must be kept informed by fact sheets and word-of-mouth messages from top management. Both civic and business leaders should not forget to ask for support from subordinates in a difficult time. Normally, subordinates will expect to be useful and trustworthy, but they may feel neglected, unnecessary, or even hostile if they are told nothing. A sense of pride and comradeship are best nurtured during difficult times.

Special constituencies also need to be asked for support. For public officials, groups like county commissioners, school boards and civic commissions should be asked to help or at least yield a period of forbearance. For business leaders, stockholders are a very special group. When a crisis looks very damaging, a corporate leader might be well advised to send letters to financial backers, asking for their support. Some might sell their stocks but others may feel challenged to support the company if for no other reason than to taste a bit of drama.

Handling stress can be planned. Leaders must not only think of themselves and their own well-being, they must consider those who have an interest but are not directly involved in a crisis. Leaders have a special responsibility to workers, subordinates, and sometimes families. Often there will only be time for a word or two, but that may be all that is expected.

10

SIMULATING CRITICAL INCIDENTS

Following the brilliant performances of the British Government during the Princes Gate terrorist incident in 1980 and the Falklands War three years later, Prime Minister Margaret Thatcher received a considerable amount of praise. Most commentators remarked on her decisiveness, skilled leadership, wise choices, and resolute determination. Praise was heaped on General Norman Schwarzkopf after the liberation of Kuwait in 1991. However, few of the accolades were accompanied by an analysis describing the preparation these two leaders had undergone before their moments of trial and glory. Thatcher and Schwarzkopf were known for their personal attendance and participation in war-games, simulations in which they were forced to make mock decisions and submit their judgments to the critiques of referees and game-controllers. The American general and the British political leader had something in common. Before crises had occurred, both had rehearsed their subordinates, reviewed their emergency communications arrangements, and reevaluated their own decision-making procedures. In some measure, the achievements of Mrs. Thatcher and General Schwarzkopf in times of stress, were not surprising. Like superior athletes, they had practiced before they performed.[47]

Performance can be sharpened by knowledge and training. Each year, the Federal Emergency Management Agency and other federal institutions train hundreds of local and state officials in coping with emergencies like natural disasters and radiological and hazardous material contaminations.[48] Similarly, the University of Illinois at Chicago conducts a month-long executive development course for corporate and public officials. The course focuses on critical incident management, and training is aimed at developing the management skills necessary for people in an organization to deal with a sudden, threatening event. For instructors, the University invites American and foreign practitioners and experts from the legal, communications, law enforcement, military, and corporate fields. The course culminates in a simulation in which people attending the course are placed under stress and required to play corporate officers in a crisis. Players are given time-sensitive, difficult decision-making tasks and are subjected to hostile television interviews. The same simulation in a brief period of instruction is also offered by the University in a separate, two-day course.

Several different kinds of exercises can test a critical incident or crisis management plan and team. The Federal Emergency Management Agency specifies four exercise categories: table-top,   notification,   activation   and deployment, and full-system simulations.   A table-top exercise is generally a round-table discussion about a selected scenario by team members who review the adequacy of their plan and resources to handle a hypothetical situation. The notification exercise is usually limited to a communications check, testing the alert and warning procedures specified in the plan. Often, the notification is done on a surprise basis, and either produces confidence or doubt as to whether team members and important officers can be contacted quickly. The notification exercise is an excellent means occasionally to remind team members of their emergency duties and to update telephone numbers. An activation and deployment exercise includes the notification procedure and requires team members to report physically to their critical incident or crisis stations. Additionally, if the plan provides for the presence and readiness of certain kinds of equipment, that equipment is moved and checked for serviceability. The full-system exercise includes all of the features involved with the activation and deployment exercise but also requires a simulated incident or crisis.[49] Exercises can be conducted on an announced basis when team members and participants will know in advance when the exercise is to be held. Exercises may also be unannounced. For instance, a CEO, mayor, or chief of police may want to know how long team members will take to arrive at their designated areas and how long it will take to bring the organization to a functional status. An unannounced exercise can give those answers.

A simulation, often called a war-game, differs from an exercise, although it can be incorporated into an exercise. For example, an activation and deployment exercise may include a simulation previously prepared by appointed controllers. The crisis management team might discover they are to be involved in a war-game or simulation when they report to their emergency stations. A simulation involves a considerable amount of preparation, but it can be written and executed by company personnel without outside assistance. Essentially, it is like staging a play in a theater. Ideally, the simulation should be held at the same place an actual critical incident or crisis would be resolved.[50]

A war-game should simulate a possible, costly event. At least one study holds that high risk technological catastrophes often involve two or more potentially dangerous systems, perhaps a manufacturing facility for a toxic substance and the means of transportation for that substance. The systems might be quite safe when considered individually, but procedures at the point of transfer may be the result of years of compromises, bargains, and accommodations. As a result, safety and risk might have been neglected in favor of practical considerations to get the product from one system to another.[51]

While cautiously considering a function of two dangerous systems, a crisis audit can be made to determine the probability of a damaging incident. First, vulnerability should be analyzed. The well being of an organization might be sensitive to an international event like a change in interest rates, a natural disaster, a dissatisfied employee, a fire, an extensive computer software failure, or criminal extortion.[52] The probability of such occurrences can be calculated by first determining the number of times these events happen yearly and then analyzing the organization's vulnerability. For instance, a session with the local fire chief can produce a figure on the frequency of large fires in certain kinds of buildings. Assuming a large warehouse fire in the local fire precinct occurred every ten years and ten similar warehouses are in the district including one belonging to the organization, a one percent probability can be projected that the organization's warehouse will burn down in the next year. The risk does not increase with each year that passes without a fire—each year, there is a one percent chance of the organization losing its warehouse. Team members can then estimate what the cost will be on an average day in goods lost in a warehouse fire. They can add the costs of rebuilding the warehouse, replacing the goods, and buying new equipment. They should also add payment for late delivery and lost business due to cancelled orders. Team members then have calculated the approximate magnitude of a warehouse fire. Comparing the probability and the risk for several damaging events will determine which event or series of events might best be simulated.[53]

With an idea of which scenario might be used, a simulation or war-game can be written and played. In the University of Illinois simulation—a corporate war-game called "The Saga of Jet Oil"—a number of potentially damaging possibilities are suggested in the course of play. In this game, three or four players are assigned to single positions on the crisis management team, each player taking his or her turn at representing the group's collective decision of what should be done. Moves are accomplished at successive meetings of the crisis management team and at intervening consultation periods, approximately one hour of playing time representing a day in the scenario. Controllers maintain the general direction of progress of the game by putting into play prearranged messages like news broadcasts, court decisions, or actions of competitors. In the game, players have several options and courses they may take, and the written scenario is flexible enough to accommodate a change in corporate policy if players are prepared to recommend one. "The Saga of Jet Oil" involves some pressure on the players due to the rapid development and changing nature of the situation, the requirement for all players to deliver their recommendations in front of other players, and the necessity for the players to face pressing television interviewers to defend corporate policy and decisions. Simulation is an excellent method to test a company's crisis management plan and give a crisis action team a thorough testing. The simulation team at the University of Illinois at Chicago assists corporations and public institutions in planning and executing war-games for their employees.

Through training courses, exercises, and simulations, public officials and corporation officers can develop their skills in dealing with an unexpected incident or crisis. If funds are available, consultants can provide these services, but it is not essential to employ them to create, teach, or manage courses, exercises or war-games. With enough time and work, they can be developed by any business or group of public officials. Training courses and exercises should be conducted periodically but especially when an organization has experienced a significant turnover among its key personnel. Simulations are exceptionally helpful in detecting problems before a critical incident occurs. Successful chiefs of state, generals, and business leaders have learned to practice like athletes. They not only train their subordinates for inevitable difficulties, they train themselves. Practice might not make perfect, but it can contribute to success.

11

THE
SKILLS
OF
INTERVENTION

There is no formula for solving problems in difficult situations. However, a look at past crises reveals some useful techniques that can help. When a critical incident threatens a public or private institution, the appearance or image of that institution must be maintained, sometimes at great expense. Public information released by the institution can damage its image. Press releases must be written carefully or rereleased to correct previously released misinformation. Information should be released to the press when an issue can be redefined, when the nature of a question can be changed, or when a previous question can be answered. Direct action also affects an institution's image. The dreaded and expensive product recall, the evacuation of a city or an endangered area, the public official's resort to force to restore order, or, at the national level, the deployment of armed forces in a foreign land—these are forms of direct action. One should collect as much information about a problem as possible and then decide on direct or indirect action.

In business, the discipline of the bottom-line can assist in decision-making. Hygrade's withdrawal of its Ball Park frankfurters and Johnson & Johnson's recall of Tylenol were logical moves, especially because the products were not likely to be sold and because retailers undoubtedly would have wanted reimbursement. The two companies made costly decisions, but the alternative—keeping the products on shelves—was not cost free either. The difficult choices arose when the products were reintroduced. The companies faced options to rename the products, to consider alternative advertisement campaigns, and to create substitute products. All these choices were affected by the profit and loss projections of each company. Ultimate choices were not just related to these specific products, they had to be related to the images of the respective corporations. Although the total expense is not known, the effort to save Tylenol may have been more than the product was actually worth. However, the name of a headache remedy was not the only thing at stake. The reputation and image of Johnson & Johnson was at risk. Hygrade's predicament was similar to the crisis at Johnson & Johnson. The commercial world does have the bottom line for its activities, but the actual amount of dollars on that line is not always easy to calculate.

A public official also has a "bottom line," the fulfillment of public expectations. According to Michael Blumenthal, fulfillment may often be more apparent than actual, but objective criteria do exist concerning public accountability. During a natural disaster, for example, the public expects to be warned of dangers, updated on the situation, and, if necessary, evacuated. Citizens also expect life and property to be protected and services quickly restored after the danger has passed.

The chances for a particular intervention to work can be improved by obtaining information. In Detroit in 1967, a large menacing crowd throwing stones, forced Detroit police from a predominantly black neighborhood. A decision was made not to immediately reenter the area. The decision allowed looting to occur, but it also delayed further confrontation between rioters and police long enough to allow anger to subside. Sixteen city blocks were ravaged by fire and theft, and when police finally attempted to regain control, shooting began again. Ultimately, Army paratroopers were called into the area; forty-three people were killed, and more than 7,000 people were arrested.[54]

In Shreveport, Louisiana in 1988, riot police in a predominantly black section of the city were attacked by a crowd of 250 blacks. The officers withdrew. Fifteen city blocks were cordoned off while rioting, looting, and fires occurred. The situation was almost identical to the Detroit riot. However, Police Chief Charles A. Gruber established communications with spotters in the riot zone and began probing the area with reconnaissance patrols. By learning which blocks he could win back with minimal effort, Gruber directed Shreveport and Louisiana State police in a steady, block-by-block invasion of the terror filled streets. Soon, people had no place to run, no place to riot. Calm was restored, and although one death occurred, no one was killed by the police.[55]

The basic difference between the two civil disturbances was information. In both cases, the fundamental decisions to intervene were the same. However, in Shreveport, the police knew where and when to act with safety; in Detroit, practically no information came to police and soldiers from the riot zone. In Shreveport, Chief Gruber developed his own spotters and patrols to secure knowledge. Information improved his decision-making, and he worked to get that information.

The public expects its officials to render an honest accounting, provide a fair hearing and take remedial action. Richard M. Nixon's failure to investigate and expose the illegal activities of his supporters and subordinates is an object lesson for any public official. Before the Watergate scandal became a crisis, the President should have appointed an outside investigator, made the investigator's findings public, and fired those assistants and aides who were guilty of wrong-doing. In public office, the lack of intervention may be fatal, and activities that cannot stand public exposure are activities that lead to failure.

The right kind of intervention can change the nature of popular debate. In the Tylenol case, the initial public focus was on a poisoned product. The choice to intervene by Johnson & Johnson changed the direction of the company's crisis. After an expensive advertisement campaign, media and public attention shifted from a poisoned headache remedy to technical solutions for tamper proof packaging. Discussion moved from how to avoid being poisoned to how a company would safeguard its customers. With the use of a $400,000 satellite hook-up to thirty cities, Johnson & Johnson staged a nation-wide electronic press conference to reveal Tylenol's comeback.[56] Subtly, sympathy for the public was shifted to sympathy for a company.

Intervention usually involves action, but action does not have to be wholly defensive. Ideally, the crisis action team should consider a broad range of options, weighing one against the other in a disciplined review of advantages and disadvantages. In most cases, the selected option will have an associated cost. The team is likely to focus on how to resolve a crisis quickly with the least amount of difficulty and expense. In a rapidly changing situation, they may miss some opportunities. The leadership authority, Perry M. Smith, suggests the establishment of an "opportunities team," a group separate from the crisis action team. As a crisis occurs, the opportunities team looks for openings to gain profits and take advantage of chances to improve the status of the organization. While some must think of how to avoid disaster, others can be considering how to take advantage of it.[57]

The best kinds of intervention are those based on sound information, and good information is often the result of aggressive, carefully planned action itself. Because image and reputation are often at stake, a leader will often find that dealing with perception is just as important as dealing with reality. The leader should be given some choices as to the kinds of intervention that are available. Some good opportunities, particularly in the middle of a fast changing situation, should be used by leaders to intervene creatively.

12

PRINCIPLES OF CRITICAL INCIDENT MANAGEMENT

Fundamentally, sound critical incident management amounts to controlling events rather than being controlled by them. There is no detailed list of actions that will fit all cases, but there are some general principles and measures that have been derived from a study of past cases from both the public and private sectors.[58] First, it makes sense to be prepared for difficult times with plans and practice. Because an organization is taken unawares, the organization must continually acquire and disseminate information. Another continuing task is an analytical one—defining the scope of the potential problems. Leaders must continually answer the question, just how serious will a certain kind of crisis be?

Additionally, leaders need to select a goal for the organization to give it direction and purpose. During a crisis the leader and the team must define people and groups affected by what is occurring, and they must develop and communicate messages to each of them. The team must budget for solutions. Its main task will be to produce and choose among a number of possible intervention actions. After a crisis, the well managed organization seeks improvement by reviewing its own actions and doing whatever is needed to prevent a recurrence of the problem.

- **Plan and Practice:** A crisis and critical incident management plan answering the questions: who, what, when, where, how and why is simple to write. The basic benefit of such a plan is that it saves time. When a threatening situation occurs, time becomes crucial. The plan should envision a leader with a small number of advisors: a talented decision-making group that has been relieved of day-to-day duties to guide the organization through the crisis. The plan should be rehearsed, especially after changes in key personnel. Ideally, the rehearsal will include a simulation of a possible, costly event.

- **Getting Information:** The decision-making group—the crisis action team—will act on information. Because its decisions will be no better than its information, a flow of information must continually come to the team and must be continually disseminated among team members. It may be necessary for the team to act aggressively just to get information. The establishment of a central log book is a recommended method of pooling information and recording events. Team members should be mobile and seek as many views and sources of information as possible, avoiding a closed circle of informants who may cause paranoia and a destructive siege mentality.

' **Defining the Scope:** When a problem is recognized, a continuous effort must be made to determine the total danger posed by the problem. The scope of a threat might be expressed in dollars, lost reputations, lost lives, public scorn, or a combination of such losses. The magnitude of the problem may be of a changing nature, but that magnitude is a vital factor in choosing appropriate responses. The scope of a crisis must be known or estimated.

' **Selecting Goals:** Leaders in a crisis should determine the goals of their organization and its preferred condition. As a minimum, the crisis action team should have a firm understanding of goals so each key person is working toward the same objectives. By choosing goals, the organization's task becomes known by comparing the current condition with the preferred condition.

' **Identifying and Communicating with Audiences:** In a time of trouble, public interest can be used to further an organization's goals. A call for support and assistance might be answered by the public. The opportunity to use public interest should not be lost. However, special groups warrant unique messages. A political leader's audiences might include a legislature, a board of supervisors, or the voters in a particular district. A corporation's audiences may include its workers, its competition, its stockholders, or its bankers. Each audience may not only require its own message, it might require that its message be communicated via a broadcast, by word-of-mouth, by a paid advertisement, by letter, or by a news release.

Budget Early, Budget Often: As soon as the scope of a crisis is identified, a budget commensurate with that scope and with what can be afforded to solve the problem should be estimated. As a minimum, the budget should include figures for money and manpower, the latter expressed in working days. As the nature of the problem changes, the budget should be adjusted. The chief benefit of the budget is that it gives the crisis action team the parameters of possible interventions.

· **Choosing and Using Intervention Actions:** Conceivably, a threat might be best met with inaction, but that is not likely. Usually, a crisis action team will have to use the organization's resources to gain control of the crisis. No standard approach exists to reduce a threat, but there is a normal method of arriving at a preferred response. Several options should be considered by the team, each should be discussed in light of its advantages and disadvantages. The quality of the discussion is largely determined by the quality of the crisis action team, and outside consultants and views should be considered. The quality of a decision, however, is largely determined by the quality of the leader's decision-making style which should be vigilant but not obsessive, wary but not defensive, and firm but not inflexible.

· **Review and Prevent:** The crisis action team should review its triumphs and its failures to improve its future performance, boost its morale, reduce post-action doubts, eliminate errors, and correct procedures. At the same time, the causes of a problem should be isolated and examined. Measures should be taken to ensure the organization will not be threatened by the same problem in the future.

There is every indication that the 1990s will be an era of reduced budgets, narrow profit margins and intense competition. Although individual lives may be improved, organizations are entering difficult times, and crises will occur. However, crises usually have precursors, incidents that give warning. A sound organization will define these precursors for what they are, harbingers of things to come. The successful organization will treat these precursors as critical and take quick, effective action. By using a crisis action plan and team to resolve a critical incident, the organization is prepared to face the potential, future crisis. In the 1990s, difficult times seem inevitable, and when difficult times occur, those who prepare for them are likely to survive them.

As a postscript to this book in the Spring of 1992: Two critical incidents have been developing into crises for a political candidate, the other for a public corporation. William Clinton, the Governor of Arkansas and a Democratic candidate for the presidency, became embroiled in controversies concerning dubious charges of infidelity and of dealings with his draft board in 1969. To counter the controversy and a drop in the political polls, he and his wife, Hillary, appeared on the national television show, *60 Minutes*. He intensified his campaign in the New Hampshire primary and came in second in the vote.

In the business sector, Dow Corning came under increasing attack by the Food and Drug Administration and by women who complained about the safety of the corporation's silicone breast implants. Although the company released hundreds of pages of documents and test results on the implants, women and physicians testified before the FDA's advisory panel in Washington about the safety and dangers of the surgically implanted devices. Meanwhile, the Command Trust Network, a non-profit group in Covington, Kentucky that advises women on implants, has received thousands of calls from American women.

Dow Corning and Governor Clinton, like Johnson & Johnson and political candidates before them, are confronted with critical incidents and the problems of how to manage them. They occur everyday.

NOTES

1. Arion N. Pattakos, "Crisis: Getting a Handle on the Inevitable," *Security Management* (March 1988), 45-48.

2. The business cases—Three Mile Island, Rely Tampons, Tylenol, Firestone 500 Tires and Union Carbide—are summarized in Steven Fink, *Crisis Management: Planning for the Inevitable* (New York: American Management Association, 1986), 168-218.

3. For a discussion of change, see the thoughts of the American philosopher, Eric Hoffer, *The Ordeal of Change* (New York: Harper and Row, 1963), 1-5, 150.

4. Marion K. Pinsdorf, *Communicating When Your Company Is Under Siege: Surviving the Public Crisis* (Lexington, MA: Lexington Books, 1987), 41-42. Steven Fink, *Crisis Management,* 67-69.

5. Roger L. Kemp, "The Public Official's Role in Emergency Management," *The Police Chief* (June 1985), 42-43.

6. John Sedgwick, "Strong but Sensitive," *Atlantic* (April 1991), 70-74.

7. The Gary Hart case is discussed by Margret Carlson, "Investigations: The Busybodies on the Bus," *Time* (August 12, 1991), 23. Geyer is quoted in Pinsdorf, *Communicating When Your Company Is under Siege,* 19-20.

8. For the Vice President's comments, see "Cold Compress for the ABA," Washington *Post* (15 August 1991), A 20. The case of America's light aircraft industry is detailed in Sylvia Porter's syndicated column, *Sunday Patriot News* (Harrisburg, PA, 17 March 1991), H 9. Justice Burger's comments appeared in "Too Many Lawyers, Too Many Suits," New York *Times Book Review* (12 May 1991), 12-13. Also see Jack Anderson, "A Thousand Points of Litigation," Washington *Post* (5 May 1991), 17 and

Ellen Joan Pollock, "Trying Cases," *Wall Street Journal* (15 August 1991), 1.

9. Richard G. Head, et al, *Crisis Resolution: Presidential Decision-Making in the Mayaguez and Korean Confrontations* (Boulder, CO: Westview Press, 1978), 2. U.S. Army Strategic Studies Institute, *An Analysis of International Crises and Army Involvement.* (Carlisle, PA: Strategic Studies Institute, 1974), 6-8.

10. J.F.C. Fuller, *Generalship, Its Diseases and Their Cures: A Study of the Personal Factor iñ Command,* (Harrisburg, PA: Military Service Publishing Company, 1936), 14-16, 32-33. 67.

11. Head, *Crisis Resolution,* 49. Peter Wyden, *Bay of Pigs: The Untold Story* (New York: Simon and Schuster), 313-327.

12. Robert F. Kennedy, *Thirteen Days: A Memoir of the Cuban Missile Crisis* (New York: Signet, 1969), 30-31, 112. Michael Dobbs, "Soviets and Cubans to Give their Versions of '62 Missile Crisis," Washington *Post* (9 January 1989), A 16. Ray S. Cline, "Nuclear War Seemed Remote," Washington *Post* (5 February 1989), D 7.

13. Robert W. Komer, *Bureaucracy Does Its Thing: Institutional Constraints on U.S.-GVN Performance in Vietnam* (Santa Monica, CA: Rand Corporation, 1973).

14. Head, *Crisis Resolution*, 83.

15. The discussion of matrix management is generally from Robert F. Littlejohn, *Crisis Management: A Team Approach* (New York: American Management Association, 1983), 18-25.

16. Fink, *Crisis Management*, 67-69.

17. Head, *Crisis Resolution*, 47.

18. For the public relations aspects of the Tylenol case, see MarionK. Pinsdorf, *Communicating When Your Company Is under Siege: Surviving the Public Crisis* (Lexington, MA: Lexington Books,1987), 49-51. Other aspects are revealed in Fink, *Crisis Management*, 203-218.

19. Pinsdorf, *Communicating When Your Company Is under Siege,131.*

20. Fink, *Crisis Management*, 130-141. Pinsdorf, *Communicating When Your Company Is under Siege,* 101. Kennedy, *Thirteen Days*, 112.

21. Perry M. Smith, *Taking Charge: A Practical Guide for Leaders* (Washington, D.C.: National Defense University Press, 1986), 56. Kennedy, *Thirteen Days*, 112. Littlejohn, *Crisis Management: A Team Approach*, 28.

22. Gerald C. Meyers with John Holusha, *When It Hits the Fan: Managing the Nine Crises of Business* (Boston: Houghton Mifflin Co., 1986), 193-194.

23. This account of Lyndon B. Johnson is from William E. DePuy, *Changing an Army: An Oral History of General William E. DePuy* (Carlisle, PA: U.S. Army Military History Institute, 1986), 169-170.

24. Fink, *Crisis Management*, 157-159.

25. Fink, *Crisis Management* 69.

26. Discussions of foreign risk assessments and foreign consultants are contained in R. J. Rummel and David A. Heenan, "How Multinationals Analyze Political Risk," *Harvard Business Review* (January-February, 1978), 67-76 and William D. Coplin and Michael K. O'Leary, "Forecasting Risk in the International Marketplace," *Security Management* (August 1983), 81-87.

27. Fink, *Crisis Management*, 69.

28. Kemp, "The Public Official's Role," 42. Lars Nylen and Orjan Hultaker, "Communications in Disaster Situations," *The Police Chief*, (June 1987), 29.

29. Pinsdorf, *Communicating*, 3.

30. Fink, *Crisis*, 67-69.

31. Pinsdorf, *Communicating*, 5.

32. The case of the *S.S. Mayaguez* is detailed in Roy Rowan, *The Four Days of Mayaguez* (New York: Norton, 1975). President Ford's motivations, actions, and public approval ratings are found in Head, *Crisis Resolution*, 107-147.

33. Pinsdorf, *Communicating*, 16, 18-20, 35-36. Mayer Nudell and Norman Antokol, *The Handbook for Effective Emergency and Crisis Management* (Lexington, MA: Lexington Books, 1988), 64.

34. Brian Winston, *Misunderstanding Media* (Cambridge, MA: Harvard University Press, 1986), 1. Pinsdorf, *Communicating*, 23.

35. Pinsdorf, *Communicating*, 49-50.

36. Pinsdorf, *Communicating*, 103-104.

37. Nudell and Antokol, *Handbook*, 66. Pinsdorf, *Communicating*, 87-90.

38. Meyers, *When It Hits the Fan*, 234.

39. Fink, *Crisis Management*, 109.

40. Pinsdorf, *Communicating*, 39. Fink, *Crisis Management*, 23, 111.

41. Federal Emergency Management Agency, "Guidance for Response Team Planning," (Washington, D.C., 1985), 4-1.

42. Nudell and Antokol, *Handbook*, 77-78.

43. Smith, *Taking Charge*, 113-117.

44. Robert Levy, "Crisis Public Relations," *Dun's Business Month* (August 1983): 50-52.

45. Nudell and Antokol, *Handbook*, 130.

46. George F. Maher, "The Tragedy of Avianca Flight 052," *The Police Chief* (September 1990), 39-43.

47. Mrs. Thatcher's experience in war-games is discussed in Nudell and Antokol, *Handbook*, 116. The account of General Schwarzkopf is from the author's personal experience.

48. Federal Emergency Management Agency, "Guidance for Response Team Planning," Washington, D.C., 1985, 9-3.

49. Federal Emergency Management Agency, "Guidance," 10-1, 10-2.

50. Smith, *Taking Charge*, 58.

51. Charles Perrow, *Normal Accidents: Living with High-Risk Technologies* (New York: Basic Books Inc., 1984), 341-342, 351-352.

52. Meyers, *When It Hits the Fan*, 195-225.

53. John M. Carroll, Risk Management," *Professional Protection* (October 1983): 9-15. Littlejohn, *Crisis Management: A Team Approach*, 40-45.

54. Martin Blumenson, "Army as Cop," *Army* (May 1976), 52-54. Major General Charles P. Stone, "The Lessons of Detroit, 1967," in Robin Higham, *Bayonets in the Streets: The Use of Troops in Civil Disturbances*, second edition, (Manhattan, KS: Sunflower University Press, 1989), 185-203.

55. Charles A. Gruber, "The Lesson of Cedar Grove," *The Police Chief* September 1990), 12-14.

56. Levy, "Crisis Public Relations," 51.

57. Smith, *Taking Charge*, 58.

58. Principles for crisis action, some a bit different from the ones listed here, can be found in Steven Fink's *Crisis Management*, 24, 64, 70, 99, Meyers, *When It Hits the Fan*, 237 and Pinsdorf, *Communicating When Your Company Is Under Siege*, 43

BOOKS:

Broder, James F. *Risk Analysis and the Security System.* Boston: Butterworth, 1984.

Braestrup, Peter. *Big Story: How the American Press and Television Reported and Interpreted the Crisis of Tet 1968 in Vietnam and Washington.* New York: Anchor Books, 1978.

Charles, Michael T. and John Coon. *Crisis Management: A Casebook.* Springfield, Illinois: Charles C. Thomas, 1988.

Fink, Steven. *Crisis Management: Planning for the Inevitable.* New York: AMACOM, 1986.

Fuller, J.F.C. *Generalship, Its Diseases and their Cures: A Study of the Personal Factor in Command.* Harrisburg, PA: Military Service Publishing Co., 1936.

Head, Richard G., Frisco W. Short and Robert C. McFarlane. *Crisis Resolution: Presidential Decision-Making in the Mayaguez and Korean Confrontations.* Boulder, CO: Westview Press, 1978.

Hoffer, Eric. *The Ordeal of Change.* New York: Harper and Row, 1963.

Kennedy, Robert F. *Thirteen Days: A Memoir of the Cuban Missile Crisis.* New York: Signet, 1969.

Littlejohn, Robert F. *Crisis Management: A Team Approach.* New York: American Management Association, 1983.

Meyers, Gerald C. and John Holusha. *When It Hits the Fan: Managing the Nine Crises of Business.* Boston: Houghton Mifflin Co., 1986.

Nimmo, Dan and James E. Combs. *Nightly Horrors: Crisis Coverage in Television Network News.* Knoxville: The University of Tennessee Press, 1985.

Nudell, Mayer and Norman Antokol. *In Case of Emergency: A Handbook for Effective Crisis Management.* Lexington, MA: Lexington Books, 1988.

Peters, Thomas J. and Robert H. Waterman Jr. *In Search of Excellence: Lessons from America's Best-Run Companies.* New York: Harper and Row, 1982.

Pinsdorf, Marion K. *Communicating When Your Company Is Under Siege.* Lexington, MA: Lexington Books, 1987.

Smith, Perry M. *Taking Charge: A Practical Guide for Leaders.* Washington, D.C.: National Defense University Press, 1986.

U.S. Department of Transportation. *1990 Emergency Response Guidebook.* Washington, D.C., 1990.

U.S. Federal Emergency Management Agency. *Guidance for Emergency Response Team Planning.* Washington, D.C., 1985.

Villella, Fred J. *Risk Assessment Contingency Planning.* New York: Dimensions International, 1986.

Winston, Brian. *Misunderstanding Media.* Cambridge, MA: Harvard University Press, 1986.

Wyden, Peter. *Bay of Pigs: The Untold Story.* New York: Simon and Schuster, 1974.

ARTICLES:

Carol, John M. "Risk Management." *Professional Protection* (September-October, 1983): 9-15.

Coplin, William D. and Michael K. O'Leary. "Forecasting Risk in the International Marketplace." *Security Management* (August 1983): 81-87.

Davies, J. Clarence. "A Call for National Disaster Guidelines." The New York *Times* (9 December 1984) F 3.

Greenberg, Reuben M. and Charles Wiley. "The Lessons of Hurricane Hugo: Law Enforcement Responds." *The Police Chief* (September 1990): 26-33.

Gruber, Charles A. "Civil Disturbances: The Lesson of Cedar Grove." *The Police Chief* (September 1990): 12-14.

Healy, Richard J. "Emergency Planning: Some Concerns." *Protection Canada* (September 1980): 17-21.

Kemp, Roger L. "The Public Official's Role in Emergency Management." *The Police Chief* (June 1985): 42-43.

Levy, Robert. "Crisis Public Relations." *Dun's Business Month* (August 1983): 50-54.

Maher, George F. "The Tragedy of Avianca Flight 052." *The Police Chief* (September 1990): 39-43.

Mitroff, Ian I. and Ralph H. Kilman. "Why Corporate Disasters Are on the Increase and How Companies Can Cope with Them." *Public Affairs.* (Volume 6, 1985): 5-21.

Nudell, Mayer and Norman Antokol. "Crisis: Before the Going Gets Rough." *Security Management* (March 1988): 49-51.

Nylen, Lars and Orjan Hultaker. "Communications in Disaster Situations." *The Police Chief* (June 1987): 28-34.

Pattakos, Arion N., "Crisis: Getting a Handle on the Inevitable." *Security Management* (March 1988): 45-47.

Rummel, R. J. and David A. Heenan. "How Multinationals Analyze Political Risk." *Harvard Business Review* (January-February 1978): 67-76.

Symonds, William C. "How Companies Are Learning to Prepare for the Worst." *Business Week* (December 23, 1985): 74-75.

Universal Training Systems Co. "In Preparation for a Terrrorist Attack." *Security Management* (October 1978): 28-30.

Walsh, Timothy J. "The Team Approach to Vulnerability Assessment." *Protection Canada* (September 1990) 37- 40.

INDEX

About the Author

Rod Paschall, a free lance consultant and writer, is a 1959 graduate of West Point and first joined U.S. Army Special Forces in 1961. Commands included an "A" detachment in Vietnam, a battalion of the 5th Special Forces Group, and Delta Force. Staff assignments included the Special Operations Division of the Joint Chiefs of Staff. He is a consultant for Time-Life Books, Publications International, Inc., and the Office of International Criminal Justice. Paschall is the author of *The Defeat of Imperial Germany* (Algonquin 1989) and *LIC 2010: Special Operations & Unconventional Warfare in the Next Century* (Brassey's 1990).